Up the Winter Trail

Coastal British Columbia Stories

Wayne J. Lutz

Powell River Books

Note for Librarians: A cataloguing record for this book is available from Library and Archives Canada at www.collectionscanada.ca/amicus/index-e.html

ISBN 1-4120-8874-7

Printed in Victoria, BC, Canada. Printed on paper with minimum 30% recycled fibre. Trafford's print shop runs on "green energy" from solar, wind and other environmentally-friendly power sources.

TRAFFORD
PUBLISHING™

Offices in Canada, USA, Ireland and UK

Book sales for North America and international:
Trafford Publishing, 6E–2333 Government St.,
Victoria, BC V8T 4P4 CANADA
phone 250 383 6864 (toll-free 1 888 232 4444)
fax 250 383 6804; email to orders@trafford.com

Book sales in Europe:
Trafford Publishing (UK) Limited, 9 Park End Street, 2nd Floor
Oxford, UK OX1 1HH UNITED KINGDOM
phone 44 (0)1865 722 113 (local rate 0845 230 9601)
facsimile 44 (0)1865 722 868; info.uk@trafford.com

Order online at:
trafford.com/06-0630

10 9 8 7 6 5 4 3 2 1

To Laura...

A web designer who gives unselfishly for a good cause, including Powell River Books

---

The stories are true, and the characters are real. Some details are adjusted to protect the guilty. All of the mistakes rest solidly with the author.

Front Cover Photo:
  Heather Main, Theodosia Valley
Back Cover Photos:
  Top – Sunshine Coast Trail near Appleton Creek
  Bottom – Granite Lake

Acknowledgements

Individuals who stand by you, book after book, are the true champions of an author. When goals are long-term, it is easy to recognize your real supporters. Margy Lutz edits my draft chapters (repeatedly!) and provides the kind of quick feedback needed by an author who writes too fast and pays insufficient attention to grammatical details. Ellen Straw of Mount San Antonio College's English Department serves steadfastly as my sentence guru. Jeanne Scott of Southern Illinois University provides marketing recommendations and the encouragement needed by an aspiring author and publisher.

Ed Maithus once again assists with the book's artwork, providing cartoons that challenge my sense of direction. In some cases, his perceptions of stories lead to new directions for my chapters. And, without missing a beat, John Maithus provides endless material for my writing. It's a wonderful gift to live adventures with him and then recount them in my books. The entire Maithi clan effortlessly provides my foundation for writing. And Bro gives me the inspiration to take it easy.

During finalization of the basic manuscript, Samantha Macintyre was an important addition to my editing team, her voluminous red ink highlighting my errors and constantly improving my writing. Meanwhile, Shannon Mobley of Printorium BookWorks provided efficienct and speedy publishing assistance. Laura Mallory of the Woven Web assisted in a major redesign of my web site, an essential link in the modern world of writing and publishing.

The characters in this book are the unsung heroes of the series: *Coastal British Columbia Stories*. They live their lives with BC flavor and provide me with inspiration. They make my job simple – I merely write about what I see in them and their amazing home province.

Wayne J. Lutz
Powell River, BC
October 1, 2006

Contents

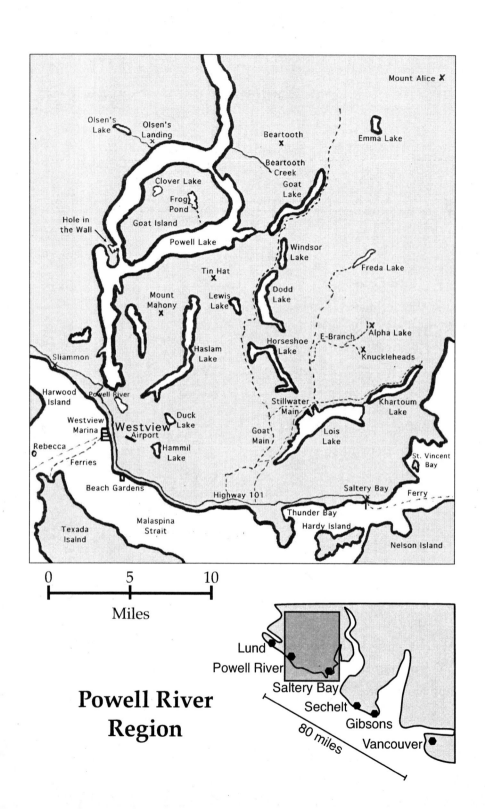

Mount Alice ✗

Olsen's Lake
Olsen's Landing
✗

Beartooth
✗

Emma Lake

Beartooth Creek

Clover Lake

Goat Lake

Frog Pond

Hole in the Wall

Goat Island

Powell Lake

Windsor Lake

Freda Lake

Tin Hat
✗

Mount Mahony
✗

Lewis Lake

Dodd Lake

Sliammon

Haslam Lake

Horseshoe Lake

E-Branch

Alpha Lake
✗

Knuckleheads
✗

Harwood Island

Powell River

Duck Lake

Stillwater Main

Khartoum Lake

Westview Marina

Westview
Airport

Goat Main

Lois Lake

Rebecca
O

Ferries

Hammil Lake

St. Vincent Bay

Beach Gardens

Highway 101

Saltery Bay
✗

Ferry

Thunder Bay

Texada Isalnd

Malaspina Strait

Hardy island

Nelson Island

0   5   10

Miles

Powell River Region

Lund

Powell River

Saltery Bay

Sechelt

Gibsons

Vancouver

80 miles

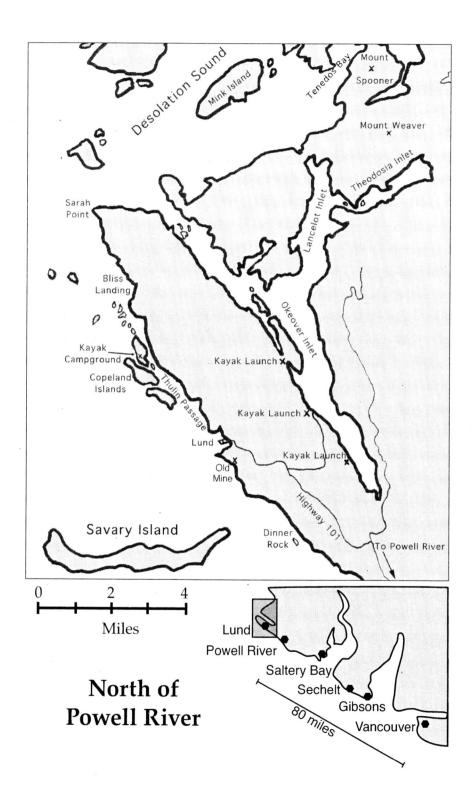

Desolation Sound

Mink Island

Tenedos Bay

Mount Spooner ×

Mount Weaver ×

Theodosia Inlet

Lancelot Inlet

Sarah Point

Bliss Landing

Okeover Inlet

Kayak Campground ×

Kayak Launch ×

Copeland Islands

Thulin Passage

Kayak Launch ×

Lund

Kayak Launch ×

Old Mine ×

Highway 101

Savary Island

Dinner Rock

To Powell River

0   2   4

Miles

Lund

Powell River

Saltery Bay

Sechelt

Gibsons

Vancouver

80 miles

North of Powell River

Preface

Canadian Visitor

When I cleared the entry gate at the Peace Arch near Vancouver, I thought I was in Canada. I was wrong. If I had continued to drive, I would have been across the border, but instead I committed the ultimate error: I pulled into the public parking area, just past the gate, and walked into the Immigration office to ask a question:

"Could you help me understand the 180-day visitor rule for U.S. citizens?" Recommendation: don't ever ask this question. There is no real answer. Worse yet, this office is the no-man's land between borders, so now the questions have been reversed on me.

"So convince me," says the steely-eyed blond woman, dressed in an Immigration uniform, her shirt covered by an intimidating bulletproof vest. "What evidence can you provide? Convince me your permanent home is in the United States."

"Well, I have a home in California, and I'm self-employed there as an author and publisher," I answer, with my best face of false confidence.

Things have shifted in the past few minutes from a few simple (I thought) questions to a decidedly defensive posture. I carry plenty of documents to verify my Canadian seasonal residence, but little to prove my U.S. permanence. A copy of the title to my house in California and my car registration would have been a nice start, but I have nothing except a U.S. passport and driver's license. Today, it is clearly not enough. I am a visitor to Canada, and the issue is to prove I am not residing there permanently.

"An author?" she asks suspiciously. "Self-employed."

A self-employed author doesn't carry a lot of official-looking documents to verify his status. I could have told her I am a philosopher seeking world peace, and it would have sounded equally valid. For a moment, I consider reaching into my backpack and pulling out a copy of one of my books. Then I decide it might make things worse – is Powell River Books a U.S. or Canadian publisher? The truth is that it is both, but I'm not sure it would settle well here. Leave worse-enough alone.

"I write stories about coastal British Columbia... In the U.S... In Canada too... But only as a visitor." Stumble, stumble – it's getting worse by the moment.

She says nothing, but gives me a stare, indicating this is not the proof she is seeking. Or maybe she is hoping for lack of proof. Is there a Canadian Immigration prison? Could I be deported for asking a question?

I reconsider the contents of my backpack, then reach in and take a chance.

"This is one of my books," I state, with an attempt at self-assurance. I slide *Up the Lake* quietly onto the counter. (Be careful not to plop it down with too much confidence.)

She doesn't touch it, but stares at the cover for a few seconds.

"Is that a garden?" she asks. For the first time, her voice is softer, even lilted. It sounds like true curiosity.

"It's a floating garden," I proudly state. "I took that photo from the front porch of my cabin on Powell Lake. If you look closely, there's a double rainbow." The Immigration officer bends over the counter to inspect the cover. It seems like genuine interest.

I reach down and flip the book over. (Slowly now.)

"And there's a picture of my cabin. A floating cabin."

"Wow." It's said without a solid sense of exclamation. But it is a definite "Wow."

I let her absorb the photo of Cabin Number 3 in Hole in the Wall. Below the photo, on the bottom of the back cover, is a picture of majestic glaciated peaks, with quad ATVs in the foreground.

"Is one of those yours?" she asks, pointing toward the quads. Is this a trick question? Is there an obscure law that prohibits Americans from riding ATVs in Canada?

"Yes, the red one is mine." I manage a fleeting moment of confidence.

"Nice," she replies. Nothing more. But I like the word.

"I write about the Powell River area… But I treat things from my perspective as an American… A visitor." Maybe I should just keep my mouth shut.

The officer continues to inspect the back cover of the book and actually smiles. I knew she had it in her. Then she looks at me, all expression immediately erased from her face. It's her turn, that moment of judgment, and we both know it.

"I'm going to type up a Visitor Record. Welcome to Canada."

A sense of relief floods over me. I feel like a prisoner who suddenly realizes he is free. You won't find me asking any more questions at the border.

Chapter 1

Little-Big Storm

As my first full-time winter in a float cabin approaches, reality starts to set in. It's really my fifth winter, but the first four don't count. Those initial stays on the float were during school recesses, brief periods in late November (U.S. Thanksgiving) and Christmas Break from my job as a college teacher. My taste of winter during those visits was memorable, with one particular snowstorm that lasted a full week. Still, it wasn't full-time winter on the float. It will be a lot different this year.

I move in during mid-September. I will be on the float for the next five months, minus several intervening trips to the States. Of course, "on the float" includes occasional overnighters in town, but this season will be nearly continual winter living in a float cabin. It will provide new challenges.

There are endless questions regarding sanity. Powell Lake cabin owners seldom stay year-round on the lake. Certainly not city-folk. What will I do during all the rainy days? Answer: As little as possible. For people who like solitude and enjoy reading and observing nature, this is the place. And not a bad place to write a book either.

Staying more than a few weeks on the float during the winter raises some logistical challenges. First, it will take a lot of wood to keep the fire going. I've been preparing the winter woodpile for months, but it is difficult to judge how much will be needed. It would be nice to expand my driftwood patrol beyond what I can pull out of the water from my deck, but that's not legal. Or is it? Certainly, cutting down trees is outside the legal boundaries. But what about a salvage license? Others have such licenses on this lake, and wouldn't that allow me to haul dead logs from the nearby sandy beach to my cabin? The tin boat could make delivery runs. A visit to the forestry office should resolve the issue.

* * * * *

I enter the Forestry District Office, expecting the worst. They won't understand, and there will be no way to properly resolve my situation. I'll be illegally pirating wood all winter, constantly looking over my shoulder, expecting to be arrested, maybe deported.

To my surprise, the clerk behind the counter treats my request politely. She even seems to understand. But she isn't sure how to handle such a minor request. I get the feeling everyone collects as much driftwood as they desire, never asking permission, and never being questioned.

I'm assigned to an administrative assistant who promises to check it out with the boss and call me back. Later that day, I listen to a voicemail that verifies I need no permit or salvage license to collect wood along the shores of Powell Lake, as long as it is not for profit. In fact, it is too easy. It would be nice to pay for a piece of paper I could carry in the tin boat when I go beachcombing, but at least it's an answer. Or is it?

* * * * *

My first full winter on Powell Lake is prefaced by a beautiful but rainy autumn. As winter approaches, a lot of what I do is in preparation for the cold – gathering firewood, winterizing the Campion (my source of transportation to and from the cabin), and changing my extravagant habits. I'll need to conserve the cabin batteries, charged by solar power, during the impending shorter days. Yet, some of the seasonal clues sneak up on me, making me question whether I am really ready for winter on the float.

On my quad, I visit Granite Lake, witnessing the autumn transition to winter. John and Eldon repeatedly cast their fishing lines into log-clogged water near our quad parking area, reeling rapidly to avoid underwater snags. John's black Labrador Retriever, Bro, waits impatiently for the odd-colored dark gray trout that reside in this lake. As John reels his line to shore, Bro chases a small fish hooked on the lure. John somehow manages to keep the charcoal-gray rainbow away from Bro, hastily releases it, and returns to fishing. Eldon and John are habitually competitive, keeping track of how many strikes, lost fish, and landed trout each accumulates. Eldon is winning.

"Do you remember when we drove our quads on that island last year?" Eldon asks John.

I don't believe him. It's some kind of a joke. The tiny island is at least 100 meters from shore.

"Sure do," replies John. By his distinct reply, I can tell John's answer is for me, not Eldon. I bite.

"You didn't have your quads on that island," I state emphatically.

How could they get their quads to that small island? Better yet: why bother?

"Yes, we did," counters Eldon. "Didn't we, John?"

"You bet." John doesn't lie, not even to pull my leg. How could this be? One end of the island is quite a bit closer to the shore, but even that part of the lake is too deep to allow crossing to the island on a quad. These machines are water capable, but they don't float, or do they?

My wife, Margy, also takes the bait: "Could you float out there, if you overinflate your tires?" Ridiculous, of course. Then again, I watched Poki and Jack a few months ago, almost up to their seats in the Eldred River. They were nearly floating.

"Nope," says John. "But it's a good guess. You should be able to figure this one out."

"Helicopter," I say, immediately recognizing my idea is ridiculous. John and Eldon wouldn't rent a helicopter for a lark visit to a tiny island.

"No," says Eldon. "Come on, this one is easy. This isn't California, you know."

"Don't give it away!" snaps John.

California. Disneyland. Eldon has been there, and Disneyland has something to do with this puzzle. Or maybe the answer has something to do with the California desert.

"You drove them to the island when the water was low," I say. No, that's not it. The water here doesn't change levels that much.

"You're getting closer," says Eldon. "This isn't California, you know."

"Stop it!" orders John. Eldon never listens to John.

"Oh!" says Margy with a surprised squeak of delight. "You drove to the island on the ice."

"Right!" says John. "I didn't think you'd ever get it. You gotta learn to think Canadian."

He's right. We don't think Canadian. This was a very simple puzzle, but my warm California world isn't surrounded by frozen water. Together, Margy and I have 50 years of formal education, but our mindset doesn't allow us to visualize how a quad can ride on water.

* * * * *

Autumn blusters in with a blast of wind and rain that lasts for days. One evening the rain stops, and there's a chance we can do something outside the next day. I extend the satellite phone's antenna and step into the bow of the Campion. I dial John's phone number, to make plans for tomorrow. The bow of the boat is a more comfortable place to sit and talk than on the cabin's deck. I must be under open sky to connect with the satellites. I've pulled the canvas back from the bow to create an impromptu phone booth. In summer, I love to sit kicked-back in the bow during my phone calls. Now it is colder, but the canvas has kept the seat dry.

After talking to John (including two dropped connections, as the satellite constellation rearranges itself), I retract the phone's antenna and step out of the bow onto the cabin's lower deck. I reattach the snaps on the boat's canvas cover, and then step up onto the raised portion of the deck. In too much of a hurry to get out of the cold and into the cabin, I catch my foot on the plastic rain gauge mounted on the lip of the deck. I tumble forward, miss the wooden-spool table by mere inches, and whack headfirst into the swim ladder.

My shoulder and head take the brunt of the blow, as I yell out in pain (and disgust). I hear the plastic remains of the rain gauge clattering behind me. It could have been a lot worse.

Margy hears the crash and my yell, and is out of the cabin in a flash. She sees me prone on the deck. I'm still yelling in spurts of anger (at myself), and I suddenly realize she doesn't know if I am seriously hurt.

"I'm okay!" I tell her.

I lie on the deck for a few minutes, calming myself down and accessing my injuries. My shoulder hurts, but nothing is broken. My head feels noticeably thumped. But I could have fallen off the deck into the water. On the way off the deck, I could have been knocked unconscious by the float's cedar log foundation. It was that close. There will be more darkness than light in the upcoming winter, and I need to be a lot more careful in routine tasks.

The next morning, under sunlit conditions, I go out and investigate the damage to the rain gauge. It's badly shattered, but modern plastic cement can perform miracles. Maybe it is a fitting forewarning of winter's dangers. It's worth remembering that rain gauges can be repaired, but humans may be more seriously damaged. It's a long way to a hospital by boat. Even Humpty Dumpty couldn't be put back together again.

* * * * *

Margy and I return to Powell River after a brief visit to the U.S. in early October. There is a noticeable difference from the weather we left here only two weeks ago. Under showery skies, we sneak in between storms in our Piper Arrow airplane. If we tried to navigate the last 100 miles a day later, we would have been waiting two weeks for the wind and rain to pass.

As I unfasten the canvas cover on the Campion at the Shinglemill Marina, the air inside the boat is thick with moisture. On the passenger seat sits "Buoy Boy," the inflatable toy racing buoy that guards the float cabin's breakwater entrance. When departing the cabin for the States, I removed Buoy Boy from his breakwater guardian position and took him along for the last ride to town. He has since resided patiently in the cold Campion, awaiting my return. Buoy Boy looks bored and ready for action, but he'll need a shot of inflated air. ("I've been sitting in this miserable boat for weeks, waiting for something to do. Something to do.")

Like the lucky arrival in the Piper Arrow, we make it to the float cabin just before the rain arrives in heavy, extended downpours. At the cabin, I leave Buoy Boy in the boat while we unload. I know he is bored from his lengthy period of inactivity. He loves his assignment of guarding the entrance to the float cabin, and he does a superb job. But it's too rainy to deploy him today – not too rainy for him, but too rainy for me.

Finally, on the third morning at the cabin, there is a temporary break in the weather. I prepare the tin boat, and launch it from the dock behind the float. The water in the lake has risen rapidly, and logs are starting to depart their stranded locations along the shoreline. I want to beat the lake to the punch. At nearby Sandy Beach, one of the few shallow beaches on this lake, nice piles of potential firewood await me.

I take Buoy Boy with me, to return him to duty. I motor over to the breakwater entrance, give Buoy Boy a quick blow job, and tie the yellow inflatable's rope to the steel staple on his floating boom. He bobs in the water, dragging his rope to the side in the gentle breeze. ("Finally, something to do! Something to do!")

Then it's off to Sandy Beach to gather some firewood.

* * * * *

October transitions into November, and the rain continues on-and-off nearly every day. More than one day in a row of sunny breaks is rare. I listen to the radio's weather forecast closely for a chance to fully enjoy the outdoors. I know that only the 12-hour forecast has any hint of truth, and even that is suspect. To rely on the long-range forecast is fool-hardy.

During a visit to town, the morning sky clears quickly (surprisingly, as forecasted), and the air is warm and invigorating. I waste no time driving north on Highway 101 to catch the Sunshine Coast Trail, near the tip of Okeover Inlet. The first part of the trail is park-like. But the path becomes overgrown as I progress farther from the road. Even though this is mushroom season, it doesn't look like this trail has been hiked for weeks. Chanterelles are everywhere, including right in the center of the trail. How could local mushroom pickers have missed this profitable route?

After hiking upward through a wide slash among a few large maples that have been spared the saw, I reach my goal – Old Gnarly. This is the largest old-growth fir on the Sunshine Coast, at least as documented in the hiking guide. The huge tree sits alone in the slash, 27 feet in girth, 8 feet in diameter. Old Gnarly's top is broken, but it still stands proud, overlooking Okeover Inlet. Yet, in a modern sort of way, the smaller second-growth trees in the surrounding dense groves seem more impressive. They strike upward from 4-foot bases to reach sunlight above the thick forest cover. Looking up at these mini-giants, their upper trunks converge into the grove's canopy. It's an awesome sight for contemporary eyes.

That afternoon, driving back to town, I hear the radio weather forecast, which includes sunny breaks for tomorrow morning. Although I had planned to go up the lake this afternoon, another night in town may be worth it. A kayak adventure in the morning might be possible.

I exhibit my distrust in the weather forecast by turning down the winding road towards the Shinglemill. It will take only a few minutes to load the boat with some of the supplies I'll be taking up the lake the next day. I'll still need groceries and items from the condo, but I can beat Mother Nature at her own game by loading some things tonight. It could be raining by morning, regardless of the forecast.

Back at the condo, I adjust the TV rabbit ears for the only weather forecast I can find. The Vancouver weatherman is skeptical regarding any major break in the rain. He describes the situation on the satellite map. A huge storm is offshore to the west, and there is a leading-edge split that looks like it will provide a short blast of rain tonight, followed by a brief respite tomorrow morning, followed by an even bigger blast. Tomorrow morning looks dicey.

Rain begins in the late evening and then stops near midnight. I awaken to more rain at 3 AM. When the sun comes up (behind clouds), the rain has stopped. The sky looks threatening, with cumulus breaks to the south and a solid black wall of clouds to the west. At the condo, I listen to the wind-rattled sailboat tackle in the harbour below my balcony.

The morning TV paints a bleak picture. Things change fast this time of year. The big storm has caught up to the smaller disturbance, and they have merged on the satellite loop into a huge mass. This blast is headed directly towards us. It isn't the rain that worries me, since precipitation only interferes with my plans for kayaking. The wind, on the other hand, can make Powell Lake formidable. It's time to get going, and try to make it to the cabin before the wind gets worse.

It's too late to miss the storm completely. Southeast gusts are already increasing, but there is no rain yet. If I skip breakfast and go to the grocery store quickly, I can be out of town in an hour. First, I call John to see if he needs help before I leave. My quad trailer has a broken leaf spring, and it sits in John's yard awaiting repair. To fix the trailer, he'll need to flip it over, so I offer my assistance.

"Not this morning," he says. "I've got a flat tire on my truck, and that gets priority." When John becomes focused on a task, he is very focused.

"Okay, I'm going up the lake as soon as possible," I explain. "The big storm is catching up with the little storm."

"Happens all the time," he notes. "Watch out for the wind. It's already picking up, and it's from the southeast."

In this area, southeast winds are the killers, roaring up the Strait of Georgia, intensifying in the narrow passage between Texada Island

and Powell River. The channel, Malaspina Strait, has a historic record of claiming boats during southeasters.

Margy and I rush through the grocery store aisles, grabbing the minimal items we need. We load the groceries into Margy's truck as the wind increases. Conditions are now barely acceptable for taking our boat up the lake.

At the Shinglemill, we load the boat quickly in increasingly gusty winds. I'm glad I had the sense to partially pack the boat the previous day. I back out of the dock and am outside the breakwater and on-plane quickly. The choppy waves keep my speed below 20 mph. I head across the lake towards the east shore, where there is some protection from the wind.

The waves are not as bad as expected. They have a short frequency, and that keeps their size under control. Small swells whap at the hull rather than whop at it – a good sign. Near Haywire Bay, I watch a boat in the middle of the channel, heading south towards the Shinglemill. I visualize a cabin owner who traveled to his float yesterday under sunny conditions, trying to coax an autumn weekend out of the weather pattern. Now, after hearing the latest forecast, he is rushing home this morning, rather than waiting until tonight. The big storm is catching the little storm, and an experienced local is headed down the lake from his cabin, while inexperienced city-folk are headed up the lake to their floating home. What's wrong with this picture?

Farther north, abeam John's Cabin Number 1, I watch two more boats near Cassiar Island, riding in-trail southbound.

"More boats than normal today," says Margy.

"Probably went up to their cabins when the sun broke out yesterday," I reply. "I bet they just heard the latest forecast."

"Some go south, one goes north," says Margy. She is on my side in this. We are prepared to spend the full thrust of winter at our float cabin, but the exodus today is disturbingly southbound. I wonder if they know something we don't?

"Looks like a big fire in Hole in the Wall today," I say as we pass Cassiar Island and enter the North Sea. I know it is not a fire, but the huge cloud that has dropped to the ground to the north looks like a pillar of smoke. It seems focused right over the Hole.

"No fire could survive the rain that's about to hit," quips Margy.

The North Sea is amazingly calm, in comparison to its normal choppiness. The autumn transition of this open area of water from its normal summer roughness is a mystery. I attribute the autumn's calm in this area to the gusty winds that whip off the nearby mountain.It leaves this open stretch of water more confused than normal. In the confusion, the waves seem to even out. In fact, I am able to push the throttle up a bit. I add a touch of bow-up trim to increase our speed to 30 mph.

The improved conditions last all the way into Hole in the Wall. As we round the bend at the green navigation beacon, the large cloud that seemed to be mushrooming up from the Hole now funnels farther north along the shoreline. Our cabin area is calm, with two small puffy clouds hugging the water in the back bay.

We dock before the rain hits. Just as we unload the last few items from the boat, a splattering of large raindrops begins. If we had departed the Shinglemill a few minutes later, we would have unloaded in the rain. Today we are lucky.

Nothing much happens weather-wise for the rest of the day. The rain continues, but it remains fairly light. I can still visualize the giant comma-shaped cloud-mass on the TV's satellite map, a wound-up low pressure center, and I'm certain it hasn't evaporated. Probably it lingers just offshore, near the tip of Vancouver Island, gathering energy and packing its isobars closer together, a sure sign of strong winds.

* * * * *

Near sunset, I step out onto the cabin deck, protected from the light rain by my hat. I hear the roar of waterfalls in front of me, against Goat Island. From my majestic viewpoint, water pours in three distinct streams, winding downward on the face of Goat. Long twists of tumbling water are interrupted by dramatic straight plunges. Just out-of-sight behind the firs to the south, an even bigger waterfall pours downward. I cannot see it, but I hear it pounding down behind the trees.

I focus my binoculars on the waterfalls, scanning from left to right across the face of Goat. I scan upward until the tumbling streams are lost in clouds near the top of the island-mountain. These waterfalls seem too powerful to dry up quickly, but I know they will vanish within a few hours after the rain stops. Even the biggest of these falls will dwindle to a trickle the day after an autumn storm passes. But there are other waterfalls in this region that persist – waterfalls that rival the most beautiful in the world. In the nearby high country, they are everywhere.

Near 11 PM, the rain intensifies. I lie half-awake, as drops splatter noisily on the metal roof. Soon after midnight, the main blast of wind arrives. Its approach brings me wide-awake. I can hear the wind headed our way, like a freight train. Distant and subdued at first, the frontal gusts arrive, swirling in all directions. A lull follows; and then another series of gusts. Each blast is bigger than the previous. The worst gusts tumble off the cliff beside the cabin, airflow redirected by the granite wall. It is these off-cliff gusts that shake the cabin the most and set it in motion. The anchor cables stretch to their limit and then suddenly grab the cabin, jerking it to an immediate halt – Whomp! It is a slow windup you barely feel; then another builds and climaxes with a sudden stop – Whomp!

The bedroom window, barely cracked open, is caught by a gust. Rain whips onto me. You know the winds are at the limits of "comfortable" when this occurs. I close the window and hang on (mentally) for the next whomp. It's amazing, in conditions like these, that the roof stays attached. I hear the metal sheets only a few feet above me, struggling against the storm. I sleep in short stints over the next few hours. Every once in a while, a "whomp" from the cables jars me awake.

At 3 AM, I awaken again to complete silence. I slip downstairs to check the outside conditions. Stepping out onto the deck, I find the air amazingly calm. I look up to see stars shining between gaps in the overcast. The winds aloft push the clouds swiftly to the north. Little-Big Storm is rapidly exiting the area. Hole in the Wall returns to tranquility.

Chapter 2

A-Branch

"That's not Mount Mahony," says John. "It's A-Branch." He's looking at one of the pictures included with a photo essay I provided for a recent issue of *Powell River Living* magazine. The photo shows John and me on snowshoes, and it's labeled "Mount Mahony."

"No way!" I state emphatically. "I remember the photo well. It was taken the day we drove your truck up Mount Mahony. Don't you remember?"

John doesn't forget anything. So that probably means, as certain as I am regarding this photo, the first chapter of *Up the Lake* is a total lie. Or, at best, a stupid mistake.

"Yes, I remember," replies John. "But it's A-Branch. No one will know the difference. Snow is snow."

"That's not the point. I wrote a complete chapter about our snowshoe trip on Mount Mahony. When you read the chapter, why didn't you tell me it was A-Branch?" Pinning an error on someone else is wise rationalization.

"Snow is snow," repeats John.

But I'm proud of the first chapter in *Up the Lake*. In fact, I selected it as the initial chapter just because I found the story so appealing. This time, hopefully, John is wrong.

* * * * *

Sometimes I exercise poetic license in my writing, but I try to keep the facts truthful. Mount Mahony is 15 kilometers from A-Branch, and that's as-the-crow-flies. In road distance, it's almost 40 klicks.

I remember my words from *Up the Lake*: "When the sky clears in Powell River, you can see the snowpack all around, but you can't get to it. Mount Mahony is the exception." It may be the exception, but it's not where the story took place, at least according to John.

I dig up a photo of John installing tire chains on his truck on the road to Mount Mahony during the same trip to snowshoe country. I show it to him.

"Where was this photo taken?" I ask. John can identify a specific spot on a road just by observing the rocks and bushes.

"A-Branch near the gravel pit," replies John, without hesitation.

It really wasn't Mount Mahony after all. It takes a lot to convince me I am wrong. Like the obvious facts.

"I need to go back to A-Branch," I proclaim. "Now that I know where we were, I need to retrace my steps."

"Why?" asks John. He tends to do that – ask questions that are impossible to answer.

"Just because," I reply. Tough question, stupid answer.

This error doesn't involve a tiny lie. In fact, it involves the entire first chapter of the first book in the series. Climbing back up A-Branch seems necessary. Then again, as John says: "Snow is snow."

"You won't make it very far," predicts John. "Rick tried to go up A-Branch last week. He didn't even make it to the gravel pit on his quad, and now the snow is worse."

"What about Margy's truck?" I ask.

"It's easier on a quad. It's all in the tires, and those truck tires won't do you any good without chains."

But I still need to get on snowshoes and tackle A-Branch. I need to write an accurate story. If I can't get there by truck, then by quad.

Snow is snow. But Mount Mahony isn't A-Branch.

* * * * *.

I know John isn't planning to snowshoe with us today. It's a Sunday, and he and Rick (Bro too!) rode all day yesterday in Theodosia. They will be worn out, so certainly an early morning is not in the cards for John today. But Margy and I awake bright and early, hook up the quad trailer, and finish breakfast. On the way out of town, although it is still only 9 AM, I have this overwhelming urge to harass John. He probably isn't even awake yet.

I ring the doorbell, and at least someone (Bro) is awake. He comes barking down the stairs. I stand on tiptoes to look through the door's high window that is more decorative than functional. I routinely conduct conversations with Bro this way, and he enjoys it. I can tell by his enthusiastic barking.

I stare through the high window and talk to Bro. Bro barks and barks. Finally, Rick stumbles to the door. If the doorbell didn't awaken him, the barking certainly did.

"Hey, how's it going?" says Rick in his normal good humor. He looks like he just woke up.

"Doin' good," I reply. "We're ready to go." Rick sticks his head out the door and sees our truck and quad trailer plastered perpendicular across the driveway entrance.

"Man, you're loaded and everything," says Rick. "What's up?"

"We're headed for A-Branch. Maybe you and John would like to join us." I'm sure they have other plans. And their plans, whatever they are, don't include a 9 AM start.

"Well, we might be gong back to Theodosia today for some trail building, but that will be a bit later. John isn't even up yet."

As I talk to Rick, I see John, wearing only long-johns, slip out of his downstairs bedroom towards the bathroom. He couldn't sleep through Bro's barking either. I jump at my chance.

"Hey, John!" I holler. "Let's get going – you're holding me up!" As John slips into the bathroom, I give him one last blast as he closes the door: "You're always lagging behind!" It's a bit of futile payback.

Rick laughs, his expression telling me he understands. John is always in a hurry to get going. It's his trademark, and he constantly harasses me about how slow I am. No one dares imply John is a slowpoke. But I try.

As I wait for John, Rick tells me about yesterday's ride. I am amazed to learn they made it so far on the muddy trail.

"It's been raining all month," I comment. "I was on that trail in the summer, and it was mud and ruts even then. It must be really rough now."

"Not so bad, if you know what you're doing." It's not a put-down to my riding skills, but just a reminder of the obvious. Rick and John aren't average riders. I can only imagine the muddy mess on that trail during the winter.

John joins us, while slipping on a T-shirt. I continue to harass him.

"So, are you finally ready to go?" I ask. "We're going to A-Branch."

"Rick and I might be going to Theo today," replies John. "If not, maybe I'll catch up to you a little later."

"It's okay – we can wait while you eat breakfast," I retort. "It will be fun rushing you along. Hey, I'd like that! Let's get moving!"

"No way!" John laughs. He knows he is always hurrying me along. We both know I need it.

"I'll stay here and bug you during breakfast." I won't let up. "Let's get going!"

"Get outta here!" John growls. So I do. But it was worth it.

* * * * *

We park on the rock-surfaced turnout at Tin Hat Junction. A logging truck and our pickup with its trailer are the only vehicles in the wide parking area. The sky threatens rain, with a forecast high of 9 degrees C. That, of course, is at sea level.

We load our snowshoes and poles on our quads and ride down to the Khartoum cutoff, taking Stillwater Main north to A-Branch. The initial climb is through an extensive logging slash, and then up into the snow.

At first, the ground is a mix of wet, crystalline snow, partially covering tire tracks in the dirt. A few vehicles have been through here lately, probably yesterday during a rare sunny day in the heart of winter.

Within a kilometer, light snow begins to fall. Since we know rain lies below us when it snows up here, we hope the precipitation will stop before we have to retrace our path back to the truck.

I lead on my Kodiak ATV, putting my right wheels in the tire track and my left wheels on the snowy center hump. There's lots of grip, until the dirt track turns white. Even then, the wet nature of the snow provides adequate climbing traction for another kilometer.

As the snow deepens, I feel my tires starting to spin. It's a slow deterioration towards lack of control. In fact, I am amazed how far we are able to progress today. I stay out of four-wheel drive so I can better judge how Margy is feeling on her two-wheel drive quad. I watch her in my rear-view mirror. She follows without apparent problem.

At a curve with a wide turnout, I consider pulling over and parking for our switch-over to snowshoes. Although my rear wheels are spinning pretty good by now, I still have plenty of forward momentum, so I continue past the corner. The next hill is challenging, but we climb it fine. At the following turnout, also on a curve, I decide we should not push our luck any further. I pull to the side of the road in trackless 8-inch deep snow and stop.

Margy pulls up behind me, with wheels spinning but still progressing slowly. It's a nice change from our typical climb-until-you're-stuck strategy. I'm sure we could not make it up the next hill, and we lose little distance by stopping here. In return, we gain a wide, secure parking spot.

As we put on our snowshoes, the falling snow produces a near whiteout. The sky is thinly overcast. Diffuse sunlight seeps through the clouds, reflecting off snow on the ground and flakes in the air. Maybe my quad goggles will help. They do! – their tinted lenses make good snowshoe goggles. I will hike with them today.

Just as we begin our snowshoe climb, we hear the sound of engines from below. We stop and wait.

A red Jeep, jacked-up with huge tires, roars around the corner. It has good momentum and excellent traction. Right behind the Jeep is a white F350 crew cab, wheels spinning and throwing snow. In the bed of the truck sits a green quad and an inflated 6-foot diameter inner tube.

The red Jeep cuts around the corner and up the next hill, but the white truck is near its limit. It spins around the curve, trying to gain traction. But it's hopeless. As it barely starts up the steep grade, the truck grinds to a halt and then starts slipping sideways. The driver backs down to the corner and gives it another try, with similar results.

The Jeep backs down the hill to assist, quickly tying a rope to the front of the truck and beginning to tow. But even with the Jeep's assistance, there is no forward progress. The towing maneuver is abandoned, and the truck backs into the turnoff near our quads. The Jeep stops in the middle of the road next to the truck. We wave to them; then we start up the hill.

"Was that a quad or a snowmobile in the truck?" asks Margy.

"Well, I assume it was a quad," I reply. "But I really didn't give it a close look. If it's a snowmobile, we'll know soon." A quad wouldn't be able to climb much higher today, so it makes sense that the truck carries a snowmobile.

Around the next corner, a gravel pit provides both a landmark and a parking area for winter climbers. Today there is only one pickup truck here.

An overnight cabin for hikers and cross-country skiers sits a few kilometers above us. Considering the steep grade, we know we won't be able to hike that far today. But it will be fun to snowshoe up the road as far as we can.

Within a few minutes, the red Jeep passes us, climbing seemingly without effort in the deepening snow. Its large tires grip well, leaving big tread marks. Then we hear another engine, so we step aside awaiting the quad-snowmobile.

It's both! – a quad with large snowcat treads, making it a pseudo-snowmobile, a baby snowcat. It passes us at about 20 klicks, showing off its solid stability. It flings snow from its big treads, while towing two teenagers who are lying prone on the huge inner tube behind it. The two boys are bouncing and sliding from side-to-side on the narrow road. The quad-snowmobile will easily make it to the cabin, maybe without throwing the tube and its passengers off the road.

We watch the snowcat disappear over the next rise and return to our trek upward. We begin to puff and pant. The sweat will be next.

"Tracks," says Margy, pointing to prints in the snow. "Could be a horse, or maybe an elk."

We stop to inspect the tracks in the snow. I suppose someone could bring a horse here in the snow. But the hoof prints go off the road, directly into the dense forest. The tracks are clear and fresh.

"Pointed toes," notes Margy. "Not a horse. Probably an elk."

"And a big one," I add. It's uniquely satisfying to visualize such a big animal passing through here only minutes before us.

We rest at the base of the next hill, and then decide to head back to our quads. On the downhill hike, two cross-country skiers with large backpacks overtake us. They are slowly snowplowing downward. The skiers stop briefly to chat, and we learn they have spent the night at the cabin above us. After they leave, continuing downhill, Margy and I discuss what a cross-country skiing experience would be like in this terrain.

"It must be tough climbing these slopes on skis," says Margy.

"I assume they use snowshoes on the uphill grade and carry their skis," I reply. "But I didn't notice snowshoes, unless they're inside their backpacks." One of the skiers carried a wide shovel, sticking out of his large backpack, but nothing else protruded.

Around the next corner, we learn the secret to climbing on skis. The two men are resting, with their skis off, preparing to hike down into the thinner snow. They don't want to damage their skis on the underlying dirt and rocks.

"Do you use snowshoes going uphill?" I ask the skiers.

"Don't need them," says one of the men. "Feel this."

He holds out one of his skis, bottom facing towards me. The surface looks like a dark green carpet. I run my hand along the bottom of the ski. It's velvet-smooth.

"Now slide your hand the other way along the ski," he instructs.

In the other direction, the feeling is completely different. It is rough, like prickly Velcro. The skier explains how the "skins" grab for climbing. Besides the skins, a release in the ski bindings allows his feet to swing upward for extra uphill leverage.

The skiers hike downhill in front of us, and we follow on our snowshoes at a slower pace. There has been more traffic on A-Branch today than I've ever experienced on similar mountain roads. Then again, there is snow in the air, and this is a winter wonderland.

And there is another obvious fact – this isn't Mount Mahony.

Chapter 3

Debris Field

The day dawns clear and crisp. The 8 AM temperature is minus one (Celsius), and the deck is covered by heavy frost. There is a faint glow in the air, as the false dawn hovers behind Goat Island. It will be two more hours before the sun pops out from the side of the ridge. The low arcing sun will then continue briefly across the southern sky, before dipping behind the trees at about 1 o'clock, just west of John's Cabin Number 2. The white orb will continue to ride behind the line of firs for another two hours, sunlight splashing weakly through the branches and onto Goat Island. Then the sun will disappear, not to appear again for another 19 hours. It is one week before the shortest day of the year, and the sun's presence within the granite-walled Hole is brief.

* * * * *

In the dim light of the early morning, I watch a debris field starting to develop in the channel directly in front of our cabin. Logs of all sizes, along with many smaller sticks, drift aimlessly in the entrance to Hole in the Wall. When the morning is nearly calm, as is usually the case, the Hole is one of the places on Powell Lake where you expect flotsam. This is particularly true on days like this, when the lake level is high. The rising water, accompanied by waves, breaks loose accumulated shoreline wood which drifts in whatever direction the wind and waves dictate. As is typical on this part of the lake in the morning, the drift is southward towards First Narrows and inward towards the Hole. It isn't a fast flow, but it's noticeable from our deck. A lot of this wood is perfect potential energy, already weather-cured by extended residence on the shore – energy awaiting capture.

The tin boat sits high and dry on the dock, and it takes some time to get it (and me) going. Besides the multiple layers of clothing that are required today, I need to pack rope, a hammer, log staples, and other essentials for this firewood collection trip. The tin boat's outboard motor is an old gem, but you shouldn't rely on it, so I pack an important piece of equipment: a satellite phone in a waterproof container.

Using a bucket, I splash some water onto the deck surrounding the boat, to make the launch from the dock easier. Margy and I push together to slide the tin boat into the water – "One-two-three, push!"

With the bow rope, I entice the now-floating boat back to the dock. We hop aboard and settle into our seats. My position is at the stern, where I give the outboard motor its customary series of rope pulls for a cold start. The engine fires on the third fully-choked pull. It's a good engine when it's in a good mood. I warm up the motor, reducing the choke until it runs unassisted, a tough chore with limited throttle control during idle. I motion to Margy to release the bow line.

When the time is right (before the engine dies), I shift into forward and quickly twist the throttle, to prevent the engine from stalling. We accelerate out and around the Campion and then out of the breakwater.

As soon as we clear the entrance, I add more throttle. I want to get up to speed before the spark plugs foul. It's a fine line between letting the engine warm thoroughly before advancing the power and facing a stalled engine that will not restart. Today I throttle-up quickly enough to get on-plane without faltering.

I maneuver the boat in a full-power winding route through the debris field, providing the old 15-horse Evenrude with a few moments to clear her plugs. Ahead, in the center of the channel, is the biggest log of all. It's not ideal for firewood, since its large girth will require splitting. But it will provide several days of winter heat. Getting to this prize requires zigzagging between other logs and hundreds of pieces of even smaller floating chunks of timber.

We circle the targeted log, to give the motor more warm-up time and to get a better idea of the log's adequacy as firewood. Then, before dealing with this log, I point the bow back towards the main section of the debris field. Margy is huddled in the front seat, facing backwards to escape the cold flow of air over the bow. Now she turns to survey the prospective crop of firewood.

I slow to idle, and the boat drifts forward through the wood and its accompanying frothy swirl of scum. Margy moves back to the middle seat on the port side, which gives her better access to the water. She'll scoop up small pieces from her side. I'll aim for larger wood for pickup by me at the stern's opposite side. Often, I am able to split the difference by aiming between smaller wood chunks on the left for Margy, while I simultaneously scoop up large harder-to-handle logs on my side.

Some logs are so big we must work together. One of us snags it, while the other uses arms to muscle the wooden hulk aboard the tin boat. Within a half hour, logs and fragments are stowed everywhere. Wood juts up and out over the gunnels, the bow, and alongside the motor at the stern.

As we troll for firewood, I keep a close eye on those logs that cannot be hefted aboard. We've become good judges of the size and weight of logs that we can manhandle, taking into account the waterlogged condition of the wood. Once in a while, we overestimate our capabilities in a piggish attempt to snag a log too big for our combined strength. In such cases, the log gets almost into the boat before we have to release it with a cold splash.

Logs that are obviously too big to harvest by our grab-and-capture method are candidates for towing. As we pass these logs, I evaluate their merits. We can only handle a few towed logs each trip, so decisions on which logs to pull are taken seriously. As we crawl past logs too big to grab by hand, Margy and I compare notes.

"Yellow cedar," announces Margy.

That's excellent for firewood, burning hot and providing a natural sweet scent. But if it must be split, and that means extra work. It's a tradeoff – potential heat energy from the log versus the kinetic energy it will take to split. The difficulty of hoisting the log onto the cabin's deck is also a factor. The ideal log is fat enough to barely fit through the fireplace door without the need for splitting. And the longer the better.

The previous summer, Margy swam out to an in-coming debris field and frog-kicked her way back to the cabin, clutching a log like a drowning swimmer she rescued. It took twenty cuts (but no splits) to prepare the log for burning. The 30-foot length of this near-perfect firewood specimen serves as a model for the ideal firewood log.

"That one will be tough to cut," I conclude, as a log slides past to the right. "Really gnarled – let's leave it."

With practice, you learn which logs will be an excessive challenge for the chainsaw and axe. You remember what a tough hunk looks like, and you avoid such logs in the future. Often, it's a combination of wood color and the swirl of the grain that provides the essential clues.

The boat is now getting so full that we ride low in the water. We discuss the remaining towable logs and select two to hook. Margy reaches into our boat knapsack and pulls out a heavy rope and two log staples. She hands them back to me. I have gathered the hammer from under the seat and another snatching rope that is always ready in the back of the boat.

I swing the tin boat against the first towable log and let her slide along the length, as I ready the hammer and a staple. Near the end of the log, I shift the outboard into neutral, position the staple, and give it a whack with the hammer. The staple sets easily, and I deliver a few more swift blows to secure it. The twang of metal meeting metal is loud and reassuring. With each whack, I feel less resonance from the hammer, as the staple pushes firmly into the wood.

Two quick loops with the rope will hold long enough to get the log back to the cabin. I tie the other end of the rope to the stern's starboard corner, in a metal corner-gap at the transom that seems built for the task. I shift into gear and twist the throttle, and we accelerate slowly away from the log. The 30-foot rope becomes taut in the water. I feel a firm jolt, as the log grabs hold behind the boat. For a few moments, the log is in control, slipping off to the side and pulling the stern with it. We plow partly sideways and partly forward for a few feet. Then the boat becomes the master, as the log straightens out behind us.

I aim at the second log we have selected and decelerate gradually as we approach, to prevent our trailing log from ramming the stern. I repeat the stapling process, and we are off again with two logs in tow. They vie for position behind the boat, their ropes becoming entangled briefly and then separating, as their towing paths settle down.

I drive without much attention to the logs. Once you get up to speed (which is only a few knots with logs in-tow), the boat rides nicely. It's amazing how little force is needed to keep a log going, once things settle down. Moving logs in the water, in general, is a low-energy process. Even huge logs can be guided through the water to a new location with very little muscle-power. The buoyancy of the water takes care of the weight.

Approaching the breakwater, I slow gradually. As the logs catch up with the boat, I shorten the ropes. I hand one rope to Margy, and I keep the other. We guide the logs, tucked within a few feet of the stern, into the entrance. Now I point the bow at the rear of the cabin, where the firewood float is waiting. We are home with a harvest of natural energy that will last us a winter's week. It isn't high-tech, but it works for us. Not bad for a few hours labor.

* * * * *

John blasts into the Hole, unusually fast. His Hourston rounds the corner from First Narrows and is pointed directly at me. From inside the cabin, I watch him round the corner, and I rush to the front deck. There are no occupied cabins in the Hole today except for ours, and this morning the debris field is minimal. In contrast to John's normal no-wake slow and considerate entry, it's a grand day for creating big wakes.

John peels off 50 feet in front of my cabin's breakwater, and angles in an arc towards his cabin across the bay. As the Hourston pulls away, I see Bro bouncing around in the back of the boat, jumping enthusiastically from side to side. He recognizes the approach to the floating cabin called "Number 2."

I watch through binoculars as the boat parks at Cabin Number 2. Through the binocs, I struggle to identify the passengers as they step out onto the dock. Bro hops out first (that's easy!), followed by Rick (probably), his friend, Monique (maybe), and finally John (definitely).

"Hey, Wayne!" John yells across the water. "Get rid of those binoculars!"

I keep the glasses focused on John, but release my left hand to wave to him. He flashes a exaggerated grin that is visible in the binoculars, as he waves back with a broad arm motion. With his keen eyesight,

John sees even better than I see through the binocs. That's 7-power magnification versus naked eyes.

I know John and Rick are planning to work at Number 2 today, continuing construction of the new cliff stairs. It's a project typical of John's heavy-duty style. They began the job last week with wood framing, and today they will work on the cement foundation.

Rick, John, and Bro immediately head towards the cliff-side construction area, and Monique takes a seat at the picnic table on the cabin's side deck. I put down my binoculars and return to my breakfast and the 10 o'clock edition of news on the AM radio.

* * * * *

After breakfast, Margy and I motor across to Cabin Number 2 in the tin boat. We are going hiking, and John can help us avoid a same-way-back route. He can shuttle us to the back of the Hole in the tin boat and then leave the boat at Number 2. We'll hike up the hill behind the Hole, join the old logging road, and then walk until we are above John's cabin. From there, we can hike down the trail that leads to Number 2 and the awaiting tin boat. A one-way hike will be a nice luxury, rather than having to retrace our steps.

When we pull into the cabin's dock, both Rick and John are busy with the sand and cement. On the side deck, we talk with Monique. We invite her to go hiking with us, but she'd rather relax on the deck. I yell over to John, asking whether he or Rick will give us a ride to the back of the Hole in the tin boat. But they are now both in the midst of mixing cement.

"I'll be awhile," John yells from the base of the new stairway. "Just can't break away right now. We need to get this cement poured before it hardens."

"Okay," I yell back. "Hey, Rick, what do you think about Monique taking us to the back of the Hole in the tin boat?" I haven't consulted Monique, of course, but I'm sure she wouldn't mind helping us.

"Well, I don't know," yells Rick. "She's never driven a boat. Ask her."

She's never driven a boat? Now that's a surprise. I assume all locals are boat people, and Monique fits my image of a hardy local. Besides, she's a taxi driver. Surely, a taxi driver in Powell River has driven a tin boat.

I glance at Monique, and she looks back at me with what I momentarily interpret as a bit of fear.

"Would you feel comfortable taking us to the back of the Hole in our boat?" I ask. She returns my gaze with what I construe as a mix of confidence and terror.

"I've never driven a boat," she replies.

Monique impresses me as the rugged type. But she doesn't look so rugged at the moment.

"Well, do you want to give it a try?" I ask. "We can practice what you need to know on the way over."

I can tell she would be happy to forget the whole thing, but there is also a glitter in her eyes that makes me think she really wants to do this.

Her answer is noticeably timid: "Okay, I guess." I wait for more, as I survey her face, trying to judge her expression. There is no more.

"Then let's go," I reply.

Margy and I assist Monique with putting on a life vest and snugging it up tight. As I yank on the straps, Monique squeaks: "Oh!" She is a small woman, and looks even tinier now, as if swallowed by the puffy yellow vest.

I help her into the wobbly tin boat, and I tell her to take the rear seat near the engine. She looks at me like I'm crazy to suggest she get this close to the outboard motor. But she takes the seat at the stern, noticeably as far forward of the engine as you can sit.

I decide she won't need to learn how to start the motor, so I'll take care of that. It is the most complex part of the whole process. Even if she flames out on her solo return, the boat carries oars.

So I plop down next to Monique, squeeze the fuel bulb, and yank the starter cord. The still-warm engine starts on the first pull.

Margy unties us from the dock, and we float next to the cabin, the motor idling in neutral. I show Monique how to turn the motor to point the nose of the boat, and I provide a quick demonstration of the gear shift lever. When the motor jerks into forward, she lets out another squeaky "Oh!"

"Try it," I say, shifting back into neutral. She carefully reaches to the side of the engine, cautiously slips the lever into forward, and then immediately back into neutral.

"Don't worry about reverse, because you won't need it," I say. "If you want to get fancy, you can try a quick burst of reverse when you come back to the cabin. But it won't hurt anything to just shift into neutral and bump gently into the dock. These tin boats are built to take it."

Monique looks at me like I'm a space invader. There is obvious horror in her eyes, so I try a bit of humor to calm her down.

"Don't worry. The Hole is only 500 feet deep," I say kiddingly.

"Five hundred feet?!" It is more of yell than a squeak.

I don't know Monique very well. But what little I know, I like. There's something about being a taxi driver in this town that impresses me. From my point of view, a female taxi driver heralds grit. Yet, her small stature stands in contrast to the job of hauling sometimes rowdy passengers from place to place. I bet she can growl, but today she squeaks.

We hover next to the dock, and Rick comes across the bridge from shore to offer words of encouragement. He tells Monique to remember to point the rear of the motor in the direction she wants to turn. That's a nice hint that makes a lot of sense to me. But Monique is in information overload at the moment. She simply stares at him.

"Hey, this will be fine," I say to Rick. "I've got tons of hours as a flight instructor. Of course, I'm not a very good one." Rick laughs, puts his hands on his hips, and watches as we prepare to launch on a journey we will later refer to as "Monique and the Tin Boat."

Under my coaching, Monique shifts into forward, and we creep out towards the breakwater opening. Now I move to sit in front of Monique, facing her. I let her do the steering. I hear Rick yell his final words of encouragement: "She can't swim, you know."

No, I didn't know. Of course, Monique knows, without being reminded. I suddenly wish I hadn't mentioned 500 feet.

We slowly maneuver out through the breakwater entrance. Monique repeatedly turns the motor the wrong way, but she catches her mistake each time, just as the boat starts veering in the wrong direction. She recovers quickly. This will work, I'm rather sure. I glance at Margy and notice a familiar look in her eyes that says: "Be careful." It is meant for me, not Monique.

Outside the breakwater, we try some turns, increasing speed a bit, slowing down, and speeding up. Pretty soon, I'm almost convinced this will work. I do wonder what will happen if Monique panics on the way back to Number 2. But John and Rick are nearby to rescue her if she drives right past the cabin towards First Narrows.

The faster speed obviously scares Monique, so we settle into a slow crawl towards the back of the Hole. In fact, this is excellent practice for her return trip to Cabin Number 2. By now I am convinced this snail's pace is the best speed to keep all of us less excited.

There are a few small logs floating in this part of the Hole, but it's not a full debris field. Monique notices a small piece of wood floating directly off the bow. She goes into panic mode.

"What should I do?!" she yells. At first I don't know what she is hollering about, but then I follow her worried stare. She's focused on a puny wood chunk.

"Ram it," I reply. "You can't hurt a tin boat."

Monique remains fixated on the tiny obstacle. I figure she will turn and maneuver around it, but she has a death-grip on the tiller. The steering handle seems welded to her hand.

She rams the wood chunk, and it thuds harmlessly off to the side.

"Whew," says Monique, with a faint gasp. Her eyes are as big as saucers, but I also detect a hint of accomplishment, maybe even a faint smile. She can handle a cab full of mill workers, but she has never experienced the challenge of a tin boat. I feel like a proud dad.

In the back bay of the Hole, we plan to use an unoccupied cabin as the docking spot to begin our hike. As we approach the cabin dock, all is well. We are pointed directly at the deck at full-slow. But now I realize I failed to tell Monique this is not the best angle of approach. At this point, parallel parking seems like a lesson way too advanced and unnecessary, so I just let her keep on trucking.

"Anywhere on the dock will be just fine," I instruct confidently. "But a short burst of reverse will make our arrival less exciting." I then remember we have not practiced reverse. But she nods, as if she understands.

We arrive at the dock at a 90-degree angle, and I wait for Monique to shift into reverse (or at least neutral), but it doesn't happen. We smash solidly into the dock. But at least we impact at a slow speed. Monique squeaks out another high-pitched "Oh!"

"See, I told you that you can't hurt a tin boat," I remind her, as I reach back and switch the motor into neutral.

As Margy and I step out of the boat, Monique looks up at me with a frail face of self-confidence. Maybe it's merely a look of disbelief that we are getting out.

"You did just fine," I say. "And the trip back will be great too." I try to believe it, as I anticipate a resistive reply. But Monique doesn't say a word. No comments either means she is ready for the return trip or she refuses to even think about it. Monique is too nice a person to abandon her to the elements of the lake, but I need to act fast before she changes her mind.

I quickly use my foot to give the tin boat's bow a smooth push. Before Monique has a chance to think about the situation any further, she is launched from the dock. I watch her eyes enlarge like saucers. Her petite yellow-vested body straightens in anticipation of the challenge.

Margy and I stand on the dock and watch Monique, as she resolutely shifts into gear. She turns the boat, and ever-so-slowly motors back towards Cabin Number 2. Monique tracks in a perfectly direct line, putt-putting away from the dock at dead-slow. I can no longer see her eyes, but I'm certain they are open wide and focused straight ahead. I yell an encouraging "Looking good!"

As the boat creeps away from the dock, Margy and I wave goodbye, even though Monique is intently focused forward.

"Bye, Monique!" I offer while still waving, hoping she will glance over her shoulder. Monique continues her stare straight ahead. She is determined to survive this horrific journey, and needless motion is not part of her plan.

Margy and I watch for the full ten minutes it takes Monique to reach the breakwater entrance. She makes the turn into the entry at a speed best described as one notch below super-slow. As she inches towards the final sanctuary of Cabin Number 2, I exhale a sigh of relief.

◊ ◊ ◊ ◊ ◊ ◊

Chapter 4

Alaska Pine

There's something about Alaska Pine. It is certainly more of a trail than a road. Alaska Pine is a steep and challenging climb for an amateur. And it possesses a certain mystique.

I first encountered Alaska Pine in the spring on a 100 cc motorcycle, when the trail was running with water. Each time I climb this path, it is a memorable journey. So when I am looking for a short ride, coupled with a winter hike, Alaska Pine is an obvious candidate.

On a cold and nearly cloudless December day, John leads Margy and me along the trail. Today will be a time challenge, since I am intent on going up the lake to our cabin before darkness falls. That requires finishing the combined ride and hike by 2 o'clock, in order to get back to town with our quads, and then to the Shinglemill before night engulfs Powell Lake. Any ride during the winter is a race against the clock. John understands our 2 o'clock goal, but he doesn't like it.

As we drive to our off-load spot near Mud Lake, Margy reminds me we cut it too close upon return from our last quad ride. We ran short of time to travel up the lake, and we barely made it before dark. After the ride, we didn't even have time to wash our quads.

"John will be upset when he sees our bikes," she says. Our mud-splattered quads ride on a trailer behind Margy's truck.

"He'll never notice," I reply. "They aren't that dirty."

"Right," says Margy. Which means John will notice. He doesn't miss a thing.

For the past few rides, I have been obsessed with tire pressure. Margy's previously low tire is holding fine, but now one of my front tires seems soft. John suggests I inflate it with my carry-along electric pump. That will be a good test of my ability to use the pump – not exactly rocket science. So at our off-load spot, I prepare to pump up the tire, while Margy slips into her rain gear. But when I push the hose fitting onto the valve stem, it doesn't seem to mate up properly.

"I'm not sure I'm doing this right," I yell to John, who is finishing the off-load of his quad, a big Grizzly, from his truck.

"Let me take a look at it," says John, as he walks over to assist. Good idea, because I obviously don't know what I'm doing.

"I don't see how that connector can push into the valve," I complain. "It's not like the inflation valves I've seen at gas stations."

"That's because the nozzle is missing," concludes John. "You're missing the whole inflation assembly. Take a look in your quad box."

Sure enough, when I search through the bottom of the box, I find a metal nozzle. I hand it to John.

"You're missing a screw and a little lever too," says John. He reaches into my quad box and immediately pulls out both the tiny screw and lever. It's as if he knows exactly where they are hiding.

While we fiddle with the nozzle, I watch Margy climb onto her quad, still parked on the trailer.

"Careful," I warn. "The ramps are pretty steep today. You can use a little brake going down." When backing down the ramps, brakes need to be used cautiously, and normally not at all. Today, however, we are parked in a position that provides a higher than typical trailer slope.

John's back is turned to Margy while he works on the valve connector. I watch her back slowly towards the ramps and align her bike for the descent. As the quad starts down, it begins to accelerate a bit more than usual, due to the steep slope. She locks her front brakes, and I watch her ungracefully slide down the full extent of the ramps. John doesn't see this, but he hears the tires slide. Without even looking up, he cringes. Now Margy is safely on the ground, and all three of us are relieved.

We finish repairs to the pump, and I fill up the low tire. Then, I start putting on my multiple layers of clothing. Today I have brought heavy gloves to go over a thinner pair.

Because of the delay with the air pump, I am now rushing to don my final layer of jacket and rain pants. The first leg of my pants stretches and snags as it slides slowly and uncooperatively over my heavy hiking boot. John and Margy sit on their quads, helmets and goggles in place, ready to ride. Bro is dressed in his blue rainsuit, waiting patiently in his aft box. All are ready, except me. Finally my other pants leg slips over its boot. I rush to pull a full-face ski cap over my head.

"Your quads are pretty dirty," notes John.

"Right," I reply. I needed that.

As I climb aboard my quad, we hear engines approaching from down the road. By the time I start my bike, four quads from the Powell River ATV Club pull to a stop next to us.

"Where are you headed?" asks John.

"Blue Ridge, if the snow doesn't stop us," says Mario. At least I think it's Mario – I still have trouble telling faces apart in their helmets.

"Nice!" says John. It's one of his favorite places, and today the snow at higher altitudes should be challenging.

I know John would like to go on a longer and more demanding ride than we have planned on Alaska Pine. So I get off my quad and walk over to John.

"Go with them," I tell him. "No problem for us."

"Nah! Alaska Pine is better for Bro anyway. He gets pretty cold when I go faster than 30 klicks in this weather, and these guys will drive fast. Alaska Pine is a nice slow climb."

I feel better about it now. John is gracious to constantly assist me, and he is the world's best guide to the Canadian wilderness. For free, of course; yet, worth a million to me.

The club's riders wave goodbye, and their four quads start up the main. A few seconds later, we are on our way behind them, but they will outrun us quickly. Bro is glad – he hates riding fast in the cold.

In a few miles, we split to the right from the road that parallels Haslam Lake, and start up Alaska Pine. At first, it is just another forest road. But it quickly narrows and becomes a trail. The gradient is immediate, constant, and lengthy. As we climb, snow appears along the side of the trail. Within another kilometer, the path is almost entirely white. Ruts from quads on previous days provide a path for our tires to follow.

We pass over icy patches that multiply as we climb higher. Recent precipitation has alternated between periods of snow and rain, so the remaining snow is crystalline. It's a slippery challenge.

John leads, followed by Margy, then me. As we approach a slick looking patch on a corner with a steep drop-off, I notice Margy slowing as she closely evaluates the trail. In front of us, John stays in the rut with his left tires, keeping his right wheels on the small center median of the trail. But I know Margy will feel uncomfortable tipped towards the downslope. She is still recovering from acrophobia (what I call quad "altophobia" in *Up the Main*, Chapter 10), but she is obviously improving from her fear of heights.

Margy selects a path that puts her right tires in the rut and her left tires on the edge of the path near the drop-off. I'm surprised she picks this alternative. She creeps upward slowly but surely, with a moment of precarious skidding. I follow, but choose to stay away from the edge, with my left tires in the rut.

Usually I stay in two-wheel drive as much as possible when riding with Margy. This way I can better empathize with her trail conditions and know when she is reaching her limit, since her small bike doesn't have four-wheel drive. But after this difficult portion of the climb, I stop and shift into four-wheel drive. It's that kind of a climb. Since Margy is doing fine so far with two-wheel drive, I may as well take advantage of what I have.

At one particularly tough spot, John stops and carefully checks the depth of water in a partially-frozen pool that stretches across the trail. Then he slowly pushes through the mix of foot-deep water and thin surface ice. John is in four-wheel drive now, and he easily shatters the ice and climbs over a small log on the other side of the puddle.

Margy enters the pool behind John, with plates of cracked ice floating in the water around her. All is well until she reaches the log. Without four-wheel drive, it is difficult to scale such obstacles without a running start.

The first try brings her to an abrupt stop. She backs away and tries again. And again, and again. John has stopped in front of us to await the results. He stands on his quad, his torso twisted around to watch. I sit on my Kodiak behind Margy, also watching. I raise my arm over my head and pump my fist, and John nods in agreement.

Finally, Margy backs up a bit farther and makes a hard run at the log. Water sprays away from her quad like a boat plowing through waves, and she roars up and over the log. John raises both hands over his head in a clasp of victory.

The climb continues, and the snow gets deeper. It is nearly a foot deep off to the side of the trail, but run-off down the path has melted it to only a few inches. Suddenly, we are in softer snow, almost powder, and the grip of our tires becomes distinctively better. It's a winter postcard: trees overhang the trail, their branches covered with snow.

Alaska Pine now levels significantly, and spits out onto a logging road. From here, John leads us to an almost unidentifiable turn-off to March Lake. We stop at the entry.

"This trail goes all the way to the lake, but it gets tough at the end," says John. "We'll ride just part way, and hike the rest."

"Sounds good," I reply. If John considers part of this path tough, it's tough.

When the going begins to get rough, John finds an area where we can pull off the trail. He stops and backs his Grizzly to the right side, into a small opening between trees. Margy takes the more-open spot to the left. There's not much room remaining, so I stop in the middle of the trail and turn off my engine.

"You shouldn't park there," says John. "That blocks the trail, though I doubt anyone else will try to get through today."

"You're right. I should have thought about that." But I did think about it, and it seems highly unlikely that anyone else will try this trail today. Still, it is a good practice not to block the path. In a series of backing maneuvers, I move my quad into an acceptable spot, clear of the trail.

It's a good thing we don't take our bikes any further on the trail today, because the walk down to the lake passes through deeply rutted terrain. At one point, John stops to inspect a large boulder that would be an obstacle for quads. He pokes at it with the pick axe he carries with him. To me, this spot is completely blocked to all but agile hikers.

"I should get rid of that rock one of these days," he says. It might require a backhoe, I think to myself.

We continue down the rough trail to an area of huge old-growth stumps, cut 50 years ago. In one extensive grove, the trunks of some of these old trees exceed two meters.

"This is the only place I've ever been lost," says John. "Rick and I hiked into March Lake before there was a trail, but on the way out we couldn't find our entry path and began veering to the right." He pauses, probably wondering if we want to hear more. We do, of course.

"Was that when you rode a motorcycle, before you had your quad?" asks Margy.

"We were in my truck that day, parked on the road. We walked down from there, but we didn't use trail-marking tape. Now I'll never hike off an established trail again without it. We finally ended up at Nanton Lake."

"Man, that's a long way away, isn't it?" I say, not really knowing where I am.

"It's only about five kilometers, but it's really rugged going."

"How did you get back to your truck?" I ask.

"Oh, that was no problem. Some loggers picked us up on the road. They were glad to take us back to my truck."

I've never been seriously lost anywhere. I don't think being unable to find the nearest Starbucks counts. I remember getting turned around on the trails above my float cabin, but then I didn't know I was lost until I rejoined the main trail. A few minutes of disorientation doesn't match a push through the forest for 5 kilometers, without any identifiable landmarks.

The path we are on spits out into a swampy area near the lake's shore. The ground is covered with foot-deep snow among small protruding hillocks. Bro romps out onto the ice, runs in circles, and yips at the air.

"Careful here," says John. "The water's not very deep, but this is the place where we're most likely to break through the ice."

The hillocks last only a few meters, and then we're on solid ice. John takes his pick axe and swings some heavy thrusts into the ice. He chops intently, finally breaking through to water below. He takes off a glove, and reaches down into the cold water to measure the thickness of the ice.

"About five inches here," he says, extending his wet outstretched hand to me as verification of his measuring tool. Then he fills the hole in with snow scraped from the top of the surrounding ice. It will refreeze without a significant lump. You don't want to disturb such a perfect lake, even if no one else is here to enjoy it.

The lake is frozen from shore to shore, with a few pressure cracks, but no significant weak areas on the ice. John stops to cut more inspection holes with his pick axe.

"There's no danger here," he says. "This lake is only a few feet deep in most places anyway. If you fell through, you'd only get a wet foot." A cold, wet foot, over 10 kilometers from civilization.

Near the middle of the lake, at one of John's ice test spots, his axe sends a loud echo across the ice. It's a metallic reverberation, almost musical in tone. Bro is enthralled by the sound and begins to bark. His barking echoes back, and makes him bark all the more. Then he run off at full speed, comes to a screeching halt, slides a few feet, and plops down on the ice. He looks like he is taking a sun bath, oblivious to the cold.

While I take some photos, Margy and John walk over to the small, mid-lake island. It is an amazing place – one of those spots where pictures never do justice.

The hike back uphill to our quads is demanding. I feel myself sweating under my multiple layers of clothing. At our parking spot, we take a lunch break before pressing on.

From March Lake, we join the main logging road that leads to Spring Lake. At a major road junction, John guides us off to the side, where a white pickup is parked. He stops and signals Margy and me with an outstretched twist of his wrist, telling us to turn off our engines.

"I need to listen for trucks," he says.

It's a weekday, and John is worried about this short stretch of road. It's the only part of the ride where logging trucks might be hauling today.

While we wait, I pull out a map. I ask John to show me where we are and where we've been. When following John, I'm often disoriented regarding my location. John never bothers to check a map. In fact, I think he hates maps.

As John traces our path for me, we hear voices. In the distance, we watch two men walking down the center of the road. They are obviously loggers. Even from this distance, I can see their bright orange hard hats and yellow and red safety vests. That explains the pickup truck.

"Put that map away!" John almost yells at me, as if he is frightened.

"What?" I say, as I fumble with the chart.

"Put it away!" he orders crisply. "They'll think we're lost."

"But I am lost," I note. He sounds upset, so I quickly fold the map and put it in my backpack.

"We don't want them to think we need a map," says John, now calmer. "I know where we are better than they do." John is an easygoing guy, but don't let anyone catch him with a map.

The loggers greet us with a smile.

"Is that Bro?" asks the logger who has a pair of grey hearing defenders draped around his neck. "If so, you must be John."

We all laugh. It's an author's dream come true.

"I just finished reading *Up the Lake*," says the logger. My grin could light a bonfire.

Both of these loggers wear bright orange cork boots and matching heavy grey sweaters. They introduce themselves as the Fuller brothers, independent loggers with a wood lot license and a commercial sawmill.

To me, they look like twins. We talk for quite a while about float cabin construction and where to find good cedar logs.

"Are there any trucks on this road today?" asks John.

"No, nothing going on today," says Ron. "We're just out scouting for a new cut. Just like you – enjoying things." Sort of a loggers' day-off.

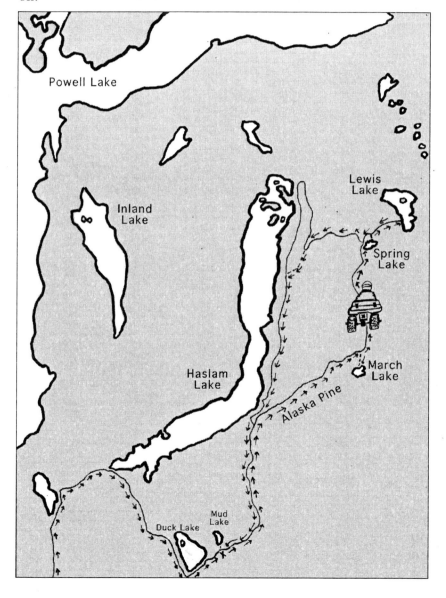

Back on the main road, John leads us to the Spring Lake turnoff, and then down a narrow trail with tightly cornered switchbacks that make the descent to the lake possible. This lake is not as accessible from the shoreline as March Lake. Fifty meters of icy hillocks separate us from the snow-covered lake ice. It's obvious you could get wet hiking out to the solid ice, so we stay on the shore. Besides, it is getting late, and it is time to go.

John doesn't have a watch, but I know he is aware of the time. It's one of his unique innate senses. I roll up my cuff and glance at my watch. It's almost 12:30, and it's quite a ways back to our trucks. To make it by 2 o'clock, we will need to start back soon.

"Let's go to Lewis Lake, while we're this close," says John.

"Okay, but it's getting late," I remark.

"It's just down the road – real close," he says. So off we go.

Lewis Lake has an established campsite, majestically perched on the edge of the lake, with a dock that extends out 20 meters into the water. You can even drive here by car. Probably not my car, and certainly not in today's snow.

Our stop here is brief. Bro is getting tired. When it is time to go, he goes over to Margy's quad and sits at the rear, ready to be hefted aboard.

"Hey, Bro – over here!" yells John. Bro reluctantly trudges over to John's quad, tail between his legs, and gets ready to be lifted aboard the Grizzly. Maybe Bro is just tired, or maybe he feels it would be easier to climb aboard a smaller bike.

On the way back down the main, John slows at the entrance to a shortcut. The entry is difficult for me to discern from the road. We ride up the narrow trail and wind through the woods in a series of sharp switchbacks. This place has the groomed look of a national park. It's one of the many trails built by riders like John. Similar to many of these routes, it's a place of piercing forest beauty.

The shortcut spits out onto the main Haslam logging road. From here, it's a nonstop run back to our trucks. The sun is getting low in the sky, and the clouds look more like snow than rain. But there is still time to make it back to town and up the lake before dark.

It's difficult to check my watch while riding, since it is tucked under the cuff of my coat. So I'm not sure exactly what time it is, but it seems like John will get us back close to our goal of 2 o'clock.

When we arrive at the truck, Margy pulls up onto the ramps of the trailer first. She drives forward, and lightly bumps the front guardrail. I drive up behind her, and stop a few inches from her quad.

Before we start strapping things down, I glance at my watch. Then I walk over to John's truck, where he is securing his quad in the cargo bed.

"That was a great ride," I state. "There's just something about the Alaska Pine."

"I like that trail too," says John.

"The only thing that would have made this ride even more perfect is if we got back closer to 2 o'clock," I taunt.

"What time is it?" he asks. Without a watch, I know he still has an uncanny sense of time.

"Three minutes to 2."

"Not bad," says John. No, not bad at all.

On the ride back to town, Margy and I decide to take an extra few minutes to stop at the car wash. The next time we ride, I'm sure John will notice.

Chapter 5

Truck Got Stuck

When my riding schedule is delayed, I am less concerned than John. He orders the part needed for my quad on Tuesday. The shop tells him it should arrive by Friday. Unlike me (skeptical American), he expects it to arrive on time. When it doesn't, he takes it personally. Even though it means I'm grounded for the weekend, I feel a bit relieved.

"Not a problem," I say. "It will probably rain anyway." True – it is March, so you can set your calendar with expectations of rain and wind. The current forecast for the weekend is clouds and showers. Besides, John's winter rides begin early in the morning, to ensure he has enough time to pack in all of the details before dark. My favorite rides are short and begin after a leisurely breakfast. So I'm not disappointed with a temporarily broken quad.

"Now they say the part will arrive on Tuesday," says John. "I'll do an oil change and lube things up while we're waiting."

"See, I knew it wasn't all bad. By the time you're finished, my quad will be like-new."

"And until then, it sits all torn apart," snaps John. I read between the lines. It isn't only the condition of the quad that is the problem.

"I bet Ed loves that," I offer. John tends to start major projects in the carport, and many of the projects are really mine. That leaves his dad's van sitting outside, in the driveway.

"He's not too keen on it, but he helped troubleshoot your quad problem." That's John's dad – a mechanical whiz, always involved. But he hates clutter. At the moment, my quad lies in pieces in the carport. And one of my trailer projects sits in the yard, a book company

miniature float cabin on wheels. "Mr. Float Cabin" sports a shake roof
and artistic brow logs, plus signage for my book company web site.

"I better not tell Ed my kayak needs hull repairs," I remark.

"No, that wouldn't be a good idea."

"We can still go snowshoeing tomorrow," I add. "Margy's truck
should be able to get us up into the snow."

"Not very well," snips John. "Without chains, you won't get far."

"But we could start into the Bunsters on Southview or Wilde Road,
and go as far as possible. Then we can snowshoe from there."

"Could," says John. "Personally, I'd prefer a quad."

* * * * *

We start up Southview Road in Margy's truck, without John. He'd
rather ride his quad today. We're determined to climb high enough
to find adequate conditions for our snowshoes. As we wind along the
southeast corner of Okeover Inlet, we pass small drifts beside the road.
At the stop sign (in the middle of nowhere), we turn right onto the
Theodosia Forest Service Road. There we begin the climb towards
upper Tomkinson Road.

This is the route that eventually loops back down Wilde Road to
Highway 101. We don't expect to get through today, due to the snow.
But we'll go as far as we can, and then exercise our snowshoes.

Margy is still getting used to the new (to her) truck. She has faced
some maneuverability challenges while attempting to back our quad
trailer into tight spots. When I provide her with meaningless instruc-
tional tips, it gets worse. Today, without the trailer, the truck rides
nicely under Margy's control. She drives the GMC at a comfortable,
moderate pace on the potholed dirt road, but she admits to being nervous about the snow ahead.

To date, I haven't sat in the driver's seat, a tribute to Margy's
tenacity. It is her vehicle, and she handles it as well as I could. But I
have more experience driving in snow, so today I am ready to assist.

The first few kilometers after the turn off Southview Road are an
indication of what is to come. Only occasional snowy patches dot the
road, but the path is rough. It is also steep and occasionally muddy,

at least by a city-woman's driving standards. We're still in two-wheel drive. If more snow is added to the mix, we'll need four-wheel drive soon. In fact, where to stop to make the change to four-wheel drive is a problem. There seems to be no letup in the steep, rutted climb. It would be best to make the switch on level ground.

I remind Margy that the Okeover lookout is only a little ways ahead. But every "little ways" we progress leads to more of the same, except the snow on the road is getting deeper.

Under my encouragement (some would call it harassment), Margy keeps the truck moving upward. The Okeover overlook finally appears on our right, and we spin out of the rutty muck onto level ground. A few inches of fresh snow in the turnout improves the traction. The lesson here is that light snow on flat ground provides better ground friction than slippery mud on a hill. But, without chains, how much snow is too much?

After a brief rest at the overlook, Margy switches into four-wheel drive. She carefully maneuvers her truck back onto the road, a tactic that requires several stops and starts in reverse and forward. I stand on the road, spotting her initial turns. I yell helpful (and annoying) instructions through her open window.

Once underway again, the road starts steeply uphill. It's an increasingly snowy surface with tracks from other vehicles. Of course, these tracks may be evidence of vehicles heartier than ours, and local drivers who know the tricks of winter driving on mountain roads.

Within another 100 meters, the road splits. The tracks lead straight ahead into what looks like a new logging slash. To the right, a road without tracks curves down to a bridge. This path is more thickly covered with snow.

Only two months ago, I rode through this area on my quad, and I don't remember this slash. Could the tracks up the hill be from logging trucks? Maybe no recreational vehicles have made it through to the main road (to the right?) in quite a while.

While we ponder the situation, Margy parks at the intersection, far enough off the road so other vehicles can pass. The snow is deep enough for snowshoes here, so we put on our shoes and strike out down the trackless road towards the bridge.

After crossing the bridge (seemingly too narrow for a main road), we hike up a small gradient that ends abruptly in a pile of logs. This is merely a spur for the logging slash and not the road we're looking for. Backtracking, we find another spur. We point our snowshoes onto it to see where it goes. Like the previous path, it too leads to a dead end. But this spur is high enough above the slash for a good view of the road with the tire tracks. That road winds upward to an obvious crest, where it angles off to the right in what looks like level terrain. Now I change my mind – this looks like the main road after all. If we can make it to the crest, it appears to be the summit of the road. If we can get to the top, we might make it all the way to the other side of the loop and back down to Highway 101.

Back at the truck, I power up my GPS to verify our position. The "You're Here" triangle shows us right on the main road. We're at a point less than a kilometer from the crest, after which the road parallels the contour lines (indicating level terrain) for another kilometer, and then starts downhill.

Looking up the road from the intersection, it is a fairly straight stretch that seems to end at a line of trees. That's where the road curves off to the right at the top of the climb. Except for the tire tracks, the road is solid white. We've already learned that the snowpack in this area increases abruptly with elevation. But I'm confident we (she) can make it.

Margy is not as confident. But she agrees to give it a try.

"What if I get stuck before we reach the top of the hill?" she asks. "How will I turn around?"

"You won't," I reply. "You'll back down to this intersection, where you can turn around."

"That's a long way to back up, going downhill in the snow," she grumbles. "Maybe you should drive."

I have no driving skills beyond hers to offer, except for a little more experience with snow and a bad case of overconfidence. We make a good team in situations like this – Margy is the worry-wart, and I'm the dare devil, by comparison. Somewhere in between is the safe and sane approach, punctuated with a sense of adventure.

"You'll do fine," I say. "Just keep 'er moving in the snow. If you stop, you'll never get started again." Wrong choice of words.

Margy does keep 'er moving, and we spin our way upward. With less than 100 feet to go, the wheels lose their traction, and the truck begins to slip sideways. But we're still inching uphill, and the crest is

ahead. I can see the road curving off to the right, as it levels at the top.
We're going to make it!

And then, with success in sight, the tires spin wildly in the snow.
The truck slips sharply to the right, and we're stuck.

"Back up a few feet, and try it again!" I yell, trying to keep my
voice under control. "We just need to make it up the final slope and
we're there!"

"How do I back up?" Margy asks. It isn't panic, but I can see her
concern creeping in.

"You might try reverse gear, while releasing the brake," I reply
sarcastically.

"I know! But I'm sideways!"

"The truck will straighten out when you start backwards," I say
confidently. Famous last words.

Margy shifts into reverse. She releases the brake, and all hell breaks
loose.

"Stop! Stop!" I yell, as the truck slides downhill at an increasingly
precarious angle. We're headed towards a deep ditch behind us, on the
left side of the road.

"The brakes don't work!" Margy hollers.

We're still sliding, but it seems we are slowing now. Yet we're slipping towards to the ditch.

"You're okay!" I state firmly. "We're just sliding on the ice. Don't let up on the brakes!"

We slide to a stop, perched at a 30-degree angle to the road, facing to the right. Our rear tires have stopped at the edge of the ditch.

"Put it in 'Park,' and set the brake," I say, as calmly as possible. "Would you like me to drive?" It is the first time I have ever asked.

The answer is an immediate "Yes!"

As we switch seats, I realize this is a heck of a time to drive this truck for the first time. In fact, this is the first time I have driven any truck. I have no special driving skills. The vehicle is precariously balanced on the edge of a ditch, and the road is covered by icy snow. The only thing I have going for me is a ridiculous case of overconfidence.

My self-assurance is so magnified that I think I can still make it up this hill. I release the parking brake, shift into forward (low, four-wheel drive), turn the steering wheel to the left, and stomp on the throttle. The tires spin and spin, and I accomplish nothing. When I release the throttle and hit the brake, the front of the truck slides a bit further to the right, making the situation even worse.

"Maybe we should try some branches under the tires," says Margy.

"Good idea," I reply. And it will give us some time to think.

We gather branches from small trees along the sides of the road. In the process, I step into the snow-covered ditch and suddenly realize how deep it is. If the branches don't allow us to pull forward, we won't be able to back down the road. By now, the truck is tilted at a 45-degree angle, with the rear tires nearly in the ditch.

I go through the scenarios in my mind. We may have to abandon the truck here, but we'll first need to purposefully put it in the ditch, to clear the road for others. John is out riding on his quad today, but he will figure out how to winch the truck from this ditch tomorrow.

I have my satellite phone, although it may not be needed. We will be able to walk back down the road, past the overlook, where other vehicles may travel today. We should be able to hitch a ride to town, or at least far enough to call a taxi.

The branches prove useless. The tires spin aimlessly. There is dirt below the snow, but we don't have a shovel. I have one last idea, valid only because it is time to put the truck in the ditch anyways.

With Margy standing outside to guide me, I apply my flying experience. Since I don't have any truck experience, it's the best I have to offer.

With Margy as spotter, I back (slide) within a few inches of the ditch, while turning the steering wheel fully to the left. The short slide sends the front of the truck further to the right – gravity in action! Then I try pulling forward, while the steering wheel is pointed to the right. There is enough traction at the edge of the road to take me forward a few feet, and the front of the truck slips even more to the right and downhill. I'm turning around!

Another reverse (steering wheel to the left) and forward (to the right), and I'm nearly perpendicular to the road. Gravity is my friend. I am slipping around with a gravity-assist. It's like trading altitude for airspeed in an airplane.

Once I hit the 90-degree point, I know I've got it made, and I'm yelling: "Yes! Yes!"

I repeat the maneuver again, and now the truck is actually pointed more downhill than uphill. We're going to be driving down this mountain after all!

* * * * *

Back on Southview Road, heading towards Highway 101, we discuss what we missed by not making it across to Wilde Road. I'd hoped we could hike part of the Sunshine Coast Trail near Appleton Creek, but that goal died when the truck got stuck. Or did it?

"Wilde Road is on our way home," I note. "We could still hike the Appleton trail today."

"Can we make it that far? Don't you think the snow will be too heavy before we get to the trailhead?"

"Don't know. But I'd like to give it a try while we're here."

You'd think optimism would evaporate after a major scare. Instead, I'm ready to plow through the snow again. After all, we now know the limitations of the truck better. This time we will turn back before getting stuck.

We turn onto Highway 101, and drive less than two kilometers to Wilde Road. From the highway, Southview and Wilde Road diverge from each other on the climb into the Bunster Range, interconnected at the top by the road we've already determined is impassible today.

We drive north on Wilde Road, to where it splits off to Tomkinson Road. As snow begins to build up, we continue past Sliammon Lake. We are still well within our driving threshold, so Margy proceeds slowly (and skeptically) up the increasing grade. We cross Appleton Creek and start up a particularly steep incline that leads to the trailhead I want to reach near a Forest Service campsite. The campground should connect to the Sunshine Coast Trail.

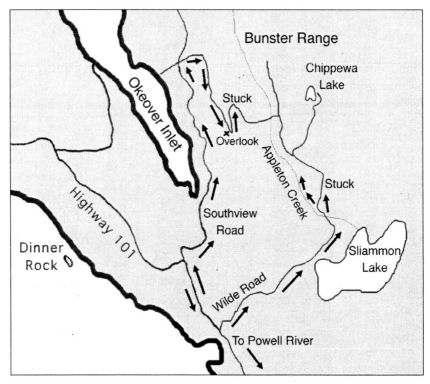

This part of the road is entirely covered by snow, marked by only a few tire tracks. It is even icier than the snow above the Okeover overlook, and soon our tires are spinning on a steep hill. Margy maintains a credible pace, but it is evident we aren't going to make it up this grade. This time she brings the truck to a halt before the vehicle begins to slip sideways. We are nearly stuck again, but we are aligned relatively straight.

"That's all there is," I sigh, admitting defeat. It takes twice to teach me a lesson. I seldom make the same mistake three times.

"Now what?" asks Margy. Though she is firmly in control of the vehicle this time, I know she doesn't want to back down this grade.

"We'll need to back down. Do you want me to drive?"

"Yes" is her simple answer. Then she adds: "We passed a turnoff right after we crossed the bridge. You can turn around there."

As I walk around to the other side of the truck, Margy gets out and positions herself in front to provide directional guidance as I back down the road. It works perfectly. At the turnout near the bridge, I back into the spur and stop.

"There's a trail right across the road," says Margy.

"I'll be darned." Sure enough, a red trail marker is firmly nailed to a tree. We walk across the road to inspect the trail. It looks elaborate enough to be a segment of the Sunshine Coast Trail. I return to the truck and dig out my trail guide.

Where we are parked marks the end of the Appleton Canyon segment of the Sunshine Coast Trail. Across the road is the Sliammon Lake continuation of the trail. In fact, the guidebook shows a dead-end parking area at this very turnout; it connects directly to the Appleton Creek section of the trail. I was headed for the upper entry point near the campsite, and didn't even know this trailhead existed. Through sheer luck (and an impassible road), we've stumbled onto the Sunshine Coast Trail.

We walk up the spur to the parking area and find the trailhead marking. The snow is considerably less deep here than at our turn-back point on the road, making the trail easy to navigate without snowshoes. Footprints in the snow indicate someone has been through this path, heading south, since the last snowfall. The Sunshine Coast Trail, although generally well-marked, is still easy to lose if you're not paying attention. Today, the footprints make the trail clear and easy to follow.

We hike along the trail (and footprints), south to north. In the summer, this would not be a good practice, since hikers traveling in opposite directions tend to meet more often than when hiking in the same direction. Thus, the standard guidebook recommendation is to hike the Sunshine Coast Trail from north to south. But in winter, there is little chance of meeting anyone on a short segment of the trail.

So we proceed northward up the trail, paralleling Appleton Creek. The creek is a raging river in winter, and its roar permeates the air. At one point, the footprints lead off the trail to the left, and we follow them to an overlook that looks down on the creek. From this cliffside viewpoint, a plummeting waterfall hits a granite shelf and splits into two falls that take the final plunge to the lower creek. This is the spot where salmon are stopped in their upward migration.

Returning to the main trail, we walk farther up the path, angling away from the creek. We hike into towering trees, mostly second-growth with a few old-growth giants near the slopes that lead down to the creek. It has taken all day, including getting stuck twice in the snow. But now we are finally here, hiking up the winter trail.

◊ ◊ ◊ ◊ ◊ ◊

Chapter 6

Up the Notch

Seasonal streams with plunging waterfalls tumble down Goat Island. They run strong during winter and spring, but have no lake of origin. The falls are created by the funneling of rainfall, snowmelt, and the occasional small spring, leaving only a trickle a few days after the precipitation ends. But when they run, they run strong. As seen from my floating cabin, the biggest funnel of them all is the Notch.

When the sun rides low in the south during December and January, the Notch lies in perpetual darkness. During these months, I've watched at all times of the day, and not a hint of sunlight enters this narrow valley, not even at midday. Just as the rays draw close to the Notch near noon, the sun begins to drop lower in the south, casting a long shadow across the gorge, and the Notch misses another day of sunlight.

I try to imagine what it would be like to be a wild animal living in this lush habitat of rain and trees during the winter, with darkness for weeks on end. I imagine hiking up the Notch, following the path cleared by the stream, to the very top of Goat Mountain.

Under the best of conditions (sunlight), it would be a demanding climb. I tried to hike another tumbling stream on Goat several years ago. I paddled my kayak to its outlet and started upward, with expectations of a simple climb. Because water cascades down this path, clearing the terrain as it flows, I anticipated easy going. I'm pretty sure-footed, but I quickly learned that mountain steams are a demanding slog. Boulders and logs are littered everywhere, pushed around by the falling water into every conceivable spot, all along the stream. Torrents of water cut deep gullies that make the upward climb nearly impossible. I returned to the kayak, defeated after climbing less than 100 meters.

But someday, I will climb the Notch.

* * * * *

On sunny days, when I prepare my telescope for the evening sky, I often set up my tripod on the cabin deck early in the morning. This allows me to check for sunspots. Then, I switch the telescope's battery-powered gears to "Terrestrial." I insert an optics adapter to provide an erect image, since astronomical telescopes portray images that are either upside-down or reversed, depending on design. With a wide-angle, low-power eyepiece, I'm now ready to scrutinize the Bunster Range, past Chippewa Bay to the west, as the mountains catch the morning sun.

I use the motorized controls to provide a slow horizontal scan along the top of the ridge, moving lower with each sweep. I stop at prospective open areas, where wildlife might be expected, and then move on. Within a half hour, I've surveyed many hectares of wilderness. Alas, I've not yet seen a single bear, deer, or mountain goat. But I pursue these visual sweeps with conviction. What I miss in wildlife, I gain in appreciation for the stark beauty of this remote landscape.

Later in the afternoon, as the sun dips low in the west, I take advantage of the sun-angle to inspect Goat Island. The Notch gets particular attention, although most of this mountainside canyon is out of view, covered by trees in the foreground. The best view of all would be obtained by standing inside the Notch, and someday I will.

* * * * *

It's a wonderful mid-March day. The sun has returned, after a two-week absence. There is not a cloud in the sky, and the temperature soars to 11 degrees C. After two weeks of cold rain, it feels a lot warmer than the thermometer indicates. Near noon, I walk around the cabin deck, wearing only a T-shirt and sweat pants.

The temperature has nearly peaked, but daylight is just beginning to reach the Notch. During March, the cavernous gully gets over two hours of sunlight in some spots, and today's sun is now approaching its zenith. I've been planning this hike for a long time, and I'm nearly ready to go.

I use a checklist for everything (a pilot's instincts), and I've just finished two equipment lists – one entitled "Hiking" and another labeled "Tin Boat." I've scratched a few non-essential items off the lists, since I want my backpack to be light for this hike up the Notch. Included in my hiking pack are a walkie-talkie, knife, flashlight, camera, gloves, water bottle, binoculars, and spare socks.

I'm dressed appropriately, with several layers of clothes and water-proof boots. Now I just need to leave before Margy has a chance to ponder where I'm going. I've told her how much I want to hike up the Notch, and she has tried to discourage me. Today, I don't want her to worry about me.

I've timed this well – Margy is sunbathing (11 degrees!) on the cabin's side deck. I walk past her, carrying my backpack and life vest, and hand her a walkie-talkie.

"I'm going up the Notch," I say, as if I'm going to the store for some milk. "Keep the walkie-talkie on, and I'll call when I have a clear line of sight."

"You're going where?" she asks, giving me the 'ol evil eye.

"The Notch."

"Oh." That's it – just "Oh." Maybe it wasn't the evil eye after all.

I step off the upper deck and out onto the narrow dock extension, where the tin boat has been pulled out of the water. I don't look back for fear Margy will try to stop me. She'd have to use a body tackle, since nothing else would do.

Anxious to get the tin boat into the water as fast as possible, I quickly unlock the chain on the boat's right side and untie the bow rope. Pushing the boat off the dock by myself is a chore. It barely budges when I shove rearward. So I walk along the edge of the dock, to the back of the boat, and grab the bailing container. I use it to toss some water under the boat to slicken the wooden dock. That's when I notice the stern drain plug isn't installed in its hole.

"Oops!" I say to myself. It's a good thing I wasn't successful in my first launch attempt.

After retrieving the drain plug from the boat's watertight storage box and installing it, I remind myself to slow down. I haven't used this boat in over a month – that's my excuse for forgetting the plug.

"I'll give you a hand." Margy appears out of nowhere. She doesn't mention the drain plug, so maybe she didn't notice. In any case, the help is appreciated.

"You'd better unhook that line first," she says, motioning to a rope on the left side that is still tied to the dock. No wonder the boat wouldn't budge. Second "Oops!"

Now I'm finally in the water, drifting contently away from the dock. I pull out the Evenrude's choke, check that the shift is in neutral, and set the throttle to idle. I pull on the starter rope. And I pull, and pull. There's no sign of ignition, so I push the choke halfway back in and pull some more. Then it hits me – the third "Oops!" in 10 minutes (on a journey of only 10 meters).

Margy stands on the dock, watching me pull and pull. She recognizes the problem about the same time I do.

"I'll get the gas," Margy says with a hint of disgust. From her position on the dock, she notices the absence of the red cruise-a-day gas tank. No gas, no go.

"Minor detail!" I yell to her, as she walks to the cabin for the tank. Margy just shakes her head and keeps walking.

By the time she is back with the cruise-a-day, I've used an oar to paddle back to the dock. I connect the tank's hose to the motor, give the fuel bulb a few pumps with my hand, and the engine fires on the third pull. I wave goodbye, and Margy adds some last thoughts:

"Be careful, please. Watch your footing on those rocks."

"Sure thing," I reply as I motor away. The hike up the Notch has got to go better than this not-so-perfect start.

* * * * *

By the time I reach the rocky shore of Goat Island, I'm feeling more confident. Hopefully, I've used up my stupidity for the day. Now, I'm ready to climb. It's time to put on my serious hat.

There's no good spot to pull the boat completely out of the water anywhere near the Notch's outlet. I find a recess in the rocks that will protect the boat from the wakes of passing vessels. I raise the motor, pull the front portion of the boat forward onto the rocks, and snug the bow line to a large stump.

The stream's outlet is not clearly defined. It ends in a rough delta of rocks that spreads out along 100 meters of shoreline. At the moment, there is no water flowing over the rocks, but I'm sure there's water in the Notch at higher elevations. Much of the water that enters Powell Lake flows underground at the outpouring of creeks like this one.

There are several prospective locations where I can begin the climb. Many small tributaries have cut gullies that lead to the outlet. As I gaze at the complicated pattern of the lower creek, I remember one of the items I scratched off my checklist – trail marking tape. I expected to be climbing up an obvious ravine. Right away, the path is not so obvious, and I wish I had brought the marking tape.

As I begin the climb, I encounter fallen trees and boulders strewn everywhere. These natural obstructions fill the narrow canyon up above my shoulders, providing a rough obstacle course. Many of the boulders are covered by moss, damp and slick. The logs range in condition from solid and slippery to soft and rotted. The only way to assure a firm foothold is to test every step, putting a little weight down before proceeding. It's a slow and tedious climb.

Through the trees, the lower portion of the Notch is in partial sunlight. But it gets darker as I climb higher and the walls of the canyon steepen and seem to close in on me. The water has carved out small caves that sometimes extend to the edges of the ravine. It is mid-March, near the end of bear hibernation. These caves look perfect for bears, although, hopefully, they are too wet. I wonder if bears are grumpy when they come out of hibernation? Especially if rudely awakened by a human being! I pick up a branch to use as a walking stick, and whack it at the mouth of every prospective hibernation den.

Surface water is running plentifully now. It's a babbling brook, clear and vibrant. Small waterfalls appear ahead, and the noise of cascading water increases as I push upward.

It's a slow process. I exit the stream to try an alternate route near the side, but I have to reverse course when the slope gets too precipitous. I push upward in short spurts of success and failure, with a lot of wasted energy. There's no alternative to trying a route as far as it can be climbed, always prepared to divert to another path.

The overall angle of the climb exceeds 30 degrees. In many spots it's at least 50 degrees, with occasional sheer drops. How the mountainside holds its rocky-faced composure, with water rushing down it, is beyond my comprehension. This slope seems to be well beyond the optimal geological angle of repose. Somehow, it holds up to the thunderous cascades of water, without giving in to a major landslide. Most of the time.

To continue upward, it is necessary to scale large logs that have fallen at various angles across the stream. Some I climb over. Others I pass under, and still others I walk on top of as much as possible, careful not to lose my footing. The same holds true for the larger boulders – I pass under the edge of several of them, stepping through cave-like formations, while thinking about slumbering bears.

The stream is still narrow but now rushing. I see a triple falls above me, and it seems there is no way to go higher. So I veer off to the side, finding a boulder with a log wedged above it. I try to use the rock and log to climb up the cliff and out of the ravine.

My first attempt sends me back down to safer footing in the bed of the creek. Then, I find another route that leads up the opposite side. By kicking my boots into loamy outcroppings in the cliff, I use toeholds and tree limbs to heft myself up and out of the canyon.

I emerge from the Notch into an area covered with prickly blackberry vines – "nature's barb wire," as John calls it. The vines grab at my pant legs and boots, and I try to kick them away. This is hopeless, so I use my walking stick and gloves to tear the vines away. Some I drag along with me.

I walk along the top of several logs that criss-cross over the vines, leading to a huge, smooth boulder. It's a perfect place to rest. I spread my whole body on the granite surface, lying down flat on my back. Sunlight filters through the trees, as I relax at this placid spot.

Sitting up, I can now look down at Powell Lake. In the distance is Hole in the Wall. There's Larry's cabin, and just to the right of it (with a concentrated stare) I can see Cabin Number 3 and its breakwater.

I'm less than a third of the way to the top of Goat Island. But I'm in the Notch, higher than I realistically anticipated. Different than I expected, yet it's the same. The Notch is as challenging as I knew it would be. I am absorbed by a wonderful sense of accomplishment.

The next time I look across to Goat Island from my cabin, I will feel a little more intimate with the Notch, knowing how it feels to stand within a ravine of challenging slope and comforting darkness.

◊ ◊ ◊ ◊ ◊ ◊

Chapter 7

Blow Power

Cabin Number 3's solar power system, designed by John, provides adequate summer power. But winter visits, when the sun rides low in the sky, are power deficient. Sunlight hours are short, and many winter days are so cloudy that almost no power production occurs. Over time, our daily routine adjusts for this inconvenience. We become conservative regarding the power system. Battery-powered reading lights and a variety of flashlights are fine for most aspects of our daily routine. Propane lights provide adequate general illumination.

But the satellite phone and a multitude of small electronic devices need recharging. And portable power packs require an electrical boost to keep a laptop computer running. Don't even think of charging a laptop from an AC outlet in the winter!

An upgrade to the cabin's electrical system provides considerable improvement, with plenty of summer power. More storage batteries are added. The primary concern now involves how to prepare the system for daily use during our first full winter on the float.

John consults his dad, Ed, an electrical wizard. His brother, Rick, also gets involved. Soon we have a variety of alternative ideas to consider. None are perfect. Rick comes up with a theoretical design that would harness energy from our wood stove.

"Imagine the amount of wasted power from that stove," says Rick. Sometimes you have to drag information out of Rick, one sentence at a time, so I bite.

"You're right, but how do we use it for electricity?" I ask.

Rick is a modest, intelligent fellow who often sits on the sidelines while others panic. His brain is always in gear, but he won't waste your time (and his) unless you're interested.

"Simple," replies Rick. "You hook up a steam generator, using a turbine to produce electricity. Basically, you boil water with the heat that's being wasted and use it to crank out electricity."

Simple – in theory. Winter is when the stove is running full blast, and that's when we're starved for electricity. But how do we convert theory into practice?

"So what would this thing look like?" I ask. "Sort of a pressure cooker with an output turbine?"

"Exactly," replies Rick. "Of course, you'd have to be careful of one thing." Rick doesn't want to overload me with information.

"What's that?" I ask.

"You don't want it to explode."

No, that's something we don't want it to do.

John, Ed, and Rick pursue this idea a bit further. It would be nice to locate a system off-the-shelf or to find someone who has built such a contraption. Surely, others have already explored this concept. In fact, as Margy's Internet research reveals, the concept has been investigated thoroughly. Most of the applications are industrial-size, although there is a company in Missouri that offers an almost-proven model for $5000. No one has documented small-scale use of such a system in individual homes. And there are problems, not the least of which is a tendency for wood-fired units to explode.

We kick around other ideas. An additional rooftop solar panel and more batteries are obvious choices. I acknowledge we may have to turn to that, but I want to try a different energy source first. And it must be natural. I already have a gasoline-powered generator that takes up the slack when the solar panels are inadequate for our power needs. The generator is efficient but noisy. It also consumes gasoline, something I want to avoid.

Rick recommends one of the newer small-and-quiet generators to meet our supplemental energy needs. I nix the idea because I'm obstinate about renewable energy, no matter how low the gasoline consumption of these newer generators.

I'm focused on wind power. It's a natural resource, and winter days have more wind than sun. Besides, generating electrical power at night is an intriguing concept.

"There won't be enough wind in the Hole to produce much power," says John.

"But substantial power isn't the goal," I argue. "Any additional power, when the sun is not cooperating, will help charge the batteries."

"You need at least a 10 mile-per-hour wind before you get anything," states John. How does he know this? There are few areas where John hasn't caught some information from a friend or from something he's read. But this sounds wrong to me.

"Don't you think the slightest breeze should turn the blades, especially with modern bearings and lightweight design?"

"True, it does seem so," replies John. "But you don't extract any electricity until you hit 10 mph. The electromagnets resist rotation until the wind picks up quite a bit."

John has pretty well dismissed wind as a source of power for the cabin. I try to convince him it is an experiment I want to pursue. How will we know whether it works unless we try? If it is a bust, we can head in a different direction, before winter sets in.

* * * * *

There are two windmills visible on the south portion of the lake. Driving up the lake in the Campion on a moderately windy day, I slow to inspect both of them. One is a sleek, modern design. The other is bigger and industrial-sized. Although a light wind is blowing from the south today, both stand motionless. Maybe the blades are purposely held stationary while the cabin owners are away, to prevent bearing damage. Or maybe John's 10 mph limit is an underestimate.

Ed loans me a book about alternative power sources. He is retired from BC Tel, and he's the electrical expert in the family. The book is an interesting how-to manual that explores all of the possibilities, including many energy sources we haven't even discussed. Hydrogen fusion, for example.

There is a chapter on wind power that is a bit discouraging, including reference to the 10 mph lower limit for power generation. The windmill section includes an old photo of an array of batteries – 58 of them, ganged together to meet your home power needs. Fortunately, I won't be operating a microwave and washing machine. The end of the chapter includes some particularly non-standard technologies, with a photo of a dog on a treadmill. Brody, we have a job for you.

Later that week, John and I browse for trailer parts at Canadian Tire (another project). In the middle of a display of battery chargers, a windmill sits on a metal post. It's a sleek-looking wind generator with graphite blades. This isn't a huge store, so what is the chance that a full demo model of a windmill would be on display? Maybe this is a sign.

"Look at that baby," I say admiringly. I need not say more, because John appreciates precision design. This windmill looks high-tech. The generator housing is an attractive dull gray, with long flat-black blades held stationary by a restraining strap. I slip off the restraint and give the "prop" a flick with my hand. The blades rotate smoothly, seemingly without any resistance.

"If nothing else, it will look cool at the cabin," I say.

"Yes, it will," replies John. He too appreciates cool designs.

* * * * *

Blow power begins at John's house. John fabricates a flange in a vise to mate a 6-foot metal pole to a four-by-four wood base. This is no ordinary 10-foot piece of wood. John used his sawmill to cut this four-by-four from a cedar log several years ago. Since then, it has sat in the woodpile at Cabin Number 2, awaiting assignment.

The wood is slightly warped, although barely noticeable to my eye. But it is not perfect, and John wants to straighten it. The four-by-four lies flat on the floor of the carport, under metal weights at the critical warped spot. After a week, it returns to a nearly straight configuration. In the meantime, multiple coats of gray paint are applied to the wood as protection against the elements.

"Where did you get the metal flange that connects the wood to the metal pole?" I ask. "It must have come from a huge machine." The flange looks like it came off an industrial-size boiler or a locomotive.

"Don't really know," replies John. "I just found it lying around here, and it seems to do the trick."

He also finds 6-gauge wire lying around in a nearby scrap yard. He buys 50 feet.

"We won't need the green wire," says John. "The other two will connect to the generator just fine." I visualize lightning making an easy exit to the deck through this thick wire, but John assures me there is little concern.

"We'll ground the whole thing to the water," he says.

Okay, so everything I learned about not dropping a hair dryer in a bathtub is wrong? For a floating house, there is no other alternative.

John's dad, who works on a detailed construction project of his own on a nearby bench, chimes in:

"As long as you keep the windmill lower than the peak of the roof, you'll probably be okay," he says. "If it does get hit by lightning, it'll just run down the wire to the electrical control box. Probably fry the whole thing." He has a way of saying things that leaves me wondering whether he is serious.

* * * * *

One Saturday, I sit by myself in John's den, watching a USC football game. With no cable TV at the condo, I rely on John's "stadium" for my autumn college football fix. I notice the installation manual for the Canadian Tire wind generator on the coffee table. I pick it up and thumb through it. On one page of the booklet are the technical specs, including: "Start up wind speed: 10 mph."

The manual has a series of complex-looking pen and ink electrical diagrams scribbled in the margins. These hand-drawn illustrations are captioned with text: "Not this one," reads one label. Another is marked: "Try this," below a circuit diagram that seems to be in Ed's handwriting. I'm certain the final product will not be your standard power system.

* * * * *

While I am in California, the wind generator pole goes vertical at Cabin Number 3. The four-by-four shaft base is lashed into the foundation of the cabin's cedar float. Two angled, wooden supports are added, to ensure it will withstand a hurricane. The final details of the electrical system are wired into the solar panel's battery junction box. Sun and wind will share the workload.

While John works on another project across the bay at Cabin Number 2, he watches the newly installed windmill at Number 3.

As the wind changes direction, the whole assembly pivots a bit on its mounting base. But the blades don't rotate at all.

Returning from California, the wind turbine gets my immediate inspection. As I approach the float, the blades stand motionless. But the wind is light, well below the expected first-rotation at 10 miles per hour.

During my first day back on the float, I sneak a peak around the corner of the cabin every time the wind gusts, no matter how slightly. The blades remain fixed in position. .

In the night, whenever I hear the slightest breeze, I sneak out to check the blades with my flashlight. It's early December, so wind is to be expected. But after a roaring November, December ushers in with only a whimper. For three days (and nights) I watch the blades. They remain stationary. Even the rotating base does not swing during these unusually light wind conditions. Yet, I am still confident. Wind and winter go hand-in-hand. This season will not be an exception. Pretty soon, I'll be making electricity long after the sun goes down, when solar panels are useless.

* * * * *

Hole in the Wall is the place on Powell Lake to escape wind. If you want wind, visit the North Sea, the open waters south of First Narrows. Or try mid-channel in lower Powell Lake, where Chippewa Bay Cabin Busters (CB CB'ers) hit hard during adiabatic outflow conditions. If you want calm, go to the Hole.

Crossing the North Sea, on the way to my cabin, it is almost always windy. Then, as soon as I reach First Narrows, the waves dissipate quickly. Entering the Hole, it is typically dead calm.

In early December, with the new wind generator sitting idle, the word "wind" seems totally absent from every weather forecast. Only a few weeks earlier, November forecasts threatened almost-daily wind warnings. Rain and wind have now been replaced by light rain showers on the verge of snow, with barely a breeze. We are not even close to the minimum wind speed of 10 miles per hour needed to turn the blades.

How windy is it? Small Canadian and BC flags, mounted on the cabin's porch clothesline, flutter in a light breeze. From my constant attention to the weather as a pilot and amateur meteorologist, I know the velocity is low. But I'm not sure how far we are from the windmill's expected rotation threshold. It would be nice to compare the actual wind speed to the needed rotation speed of 10 mph. If I owned an anemometer, I could compare its velocity scale to the first rotation of the wind generator's blades. Then I would know (for the future) when to expect rotation.

I remember watching a friend use a cute little digital anemometer. At the time, it seemed to be a bit of overkill, even for a weather junkie like me. Now it sounds like a practical method for comparing wind speed to blade rotation potential. Of course, there is a bit of rationalization here, since digital anemometers look so cool.

The package arrives in the mail. It is a tiny yellow plastic fan, almost frictionless, with a digital meter to register the results. I step outside on the deck, point the yellow plastic box into the wind, and register 2.8 mph. Meanwhile, the clothesline flags flutter with an inclination of about 30 degrees. So that flag angle implies 3 miles per hour. It's still well below the magic number of 10.

Two more weeks elapse, and I haven't caught the windmill in action yet. So far, the maximum wind velocity on my digital meter is 5.2 mph. On a two-day trip to town, I return to the float to find the wind generator pointing in a new direction. The position of the blades has also changed, so there has been rotation while I've been gone. This wind is sneaky.

* * * * *

Another week passes, and still nothing. On another trip to town, I return to find the blades of the windmill again rotated from their previous position. The windmill is playing with me.

When the clothesline flags begin to flutter, I step out onto the deck to check the anemometer. Flag flutter never develops into anything more than a maximum value of 6.1 mph.

* * * * *

I am returning to town today in preparation for tomorrow's flight to the States, and there is faint hope of seeing the generator blades turn before I depart.

Hope burns eternal – today's forecast is for a mix of snow and rain. Southeasterlies are expected to develop later in the day, rising to gale force tonight. It seems probable that the sneaky blades will be cranking out electrons as soon as I am gone.

The mid-day temperature hovers just above freezing. Rain begins, beating gently on the cabin's metal roof. Then the drumming stops, as the rain turns to snow. Within a few minutes, the decks turn white. Quick, call the airline – I am stranded and will not be going back to the States! I look for any excuse not to leave my cabin. Unfortunately, it is not even close to a weather crisis (yet).

In the late afternoon, I pack up for the trip back to town. I delay my departure as long as possible, in hope of arriving wind. On this lake, be careful what you hope for. Darkness is encroaching, so I must leave.

As I pull out of the breakwater, I glance back one last time at the stubborn windmill. It sits lifeless. Any hope for a glimpse of rotation will have to wait until next month.

* * * * *

That night, at my condo in town, the rain whips around the balcony, and wind whirls up Malaspina Strait with a vengeance. There is no doubt the windmill is making electricity tonight, if only I was in the Hole to watch the voltmeter and celebrate.

For the next two weeks, while I am in the States, rain and wind pound Powell River. On one blustery day during this period, John drives his Hourston to Hole in the Wall, crossing the wave-strewn North Sea, to enter a Hole that is ridiculously calm. He hopes to catch the wind generator in action, but it is not to be.

On New Years Day, just before my return to Powell River, a major storm moves through coastal BC, making the headlines in the local newspaper. Winds at Powell River hit 94 kilometers per hour, and a tree crashes onto a truck at the airport. The next day, John takes his Hourston north again, and discovers a surprising and sorry sight. The windmill sits idle in a windless Hole (not surprising nor particularly sorry). However, my tin boat rides upside-down (motor included) in the water. It bobs, nearly submerged, at an awkward angle, still attached to the cabin's dock by its security chain. The only thing preventing the drowned boat from completely sinking is the locked chain.

John retrieves my satellite phone from the cabin, and calls Rick. They discuss a way to attack the situation. By early afternoon, John has righted the boat, drained water from the Evenrude's spark plug holes, fired her up, and completed a test drive. The two-stroke design of the outboard motor probably saves it. The oil-gas mixture keeps the engine's components adequately lubricated while submerged.

That evening, John places a phone call to California.

"I wish I had a camera today," he says. "It was quite a sight. Don't do that again." How many lessons does it take for me to realize how windy it can get in the Hole during a storm?

"I'll admit I thought about the possibility," I grovel. "When I left the Hole, the firewood float was tied on the other side of the cabin. I knew there would be less stability for the tin boat, without the firewood float to secure it to."

"So why didn't you just tie the boat with a rope on both sides of the dock?"

Good question.

"Oh, you didn't do a very good job with the firewood float either," John snaps.

"I thought I tied it pretty tight," I reply. There's no way it could flip over like the tin boat.

"You shouldn't have tied that float to the swim ladder. When the wind hit, the stress from the firewood float ripped the ladder right off."

"Oh," is all I can reply.

The ladder is (was) a John-built hefty wooden structure. Pulling it off the side of the cabin required an extremely strong wind, but that's the nature of storms in the Hole. Now my favorite swim ladder will need to be repaired or replaced. John hates incompetence.

"Did you see the windmill turn?" I say, trying to change the subject.

"No, it was calm in the Hole today, but I poked the blades with a pipe pole, and they swing nice and free."

Someday we'll see the blades rotate on their own. In the meantime, these sneaky winds blow only when you're not there to witness them. They tear off swim ladders and flip over boats. But they won't let you see windmill blades turn.

* * * * *

In early January, Margy and I return to Powell River. As we motor into Hole in the Wall, the tin boat sits proudly on its dock, now secured on both sides. Stepping onto the cabin's dock, I notice the rain gauge overflowing from our two-week absence (gauge capacity: 8 inches). The windmill faces the granite cliff, motionless. Since installation six weeks ago, neither John nor I have caught these blades rotating, not even once.

The next morning, the flags on the porch flutter beyond the 30 degree mark. The wind shifts to the south and begins to gust. I hustle out onto the deck, anemometer in-hand. The windmill now points south and away from the cliff. Standing on the corner of the deck, I point the anemometer into the wind. Simultaneously, I crane my neck to watch the blades of the windmill. They begin to rotate behind me! It is a slow turn, but the blades are moving!

A glance at the anemometer shows 8.6 mph. The flags flutter at about 45 degrees for only a few seconds, and then it is over. The wind drops to 3 mph, and the blades stop, after only a few rotations. But the wind generator is caught in the act for the first time!

It happens too quickly to get an electrical reading on the voltmeter inside the cabin. But there is no doubt – it's blow power!

Later that afternoon, a warm January rain begins. It persists, with little wind, for the rest of the day. After darkness falls, I shine my flashlight out onto the clothesline. The porch flags fly at an angle suddenly in excess of 45 degrees. The wind blows strong and steady from the southeast. I hurry out onto the deck, and shine my flashlight on the windmill. The blades are moving again, winding up with a "Whoosh!" Back inside, to find the anemometer! Out onto the deck again, to measure the wind velocity – 16.9 mph! Back into the cabin – the electrical voltmeter registers a slight tick upward.

The solar panel is idle in the dark, and we're making electricity at night! I hurry out onto the deck again, run around to the back of the cabin (slow down: it's dark and slippery). I open the door to the electrical control box and flip on the inverter. Then I shuffle (slow now, before you get hurt) back inside.

I run around inside the cabin. I climb the steps to the loft, two-at-a-time, and turn on every electrical switch I can find. As the cabin lights up in the dark Hole, I yell like a madman! Maybe I am.

The voltmeter has barely budged. But the lights in the cabin burn bright. And the speakers blare Avril Lavigne songs from my iPod, into the crevasses of the night.

Chapter 8

Plantation Road

Early morning, December 20th: it is raining hard, and a gusty southeasterly is blowing. The ride to Vancouver on Pacific Coastal is nerve wracking. There is nothing worse for an experienced pilot than riding in the back of small aircraft in bad weather. The Embraer Banderante, a twin turboprop, is not a small aircraft by most standards. But it isn't a 737 either, and I hold on tight.

This marks the first day of heavy rain for the month, after a reasonably mild and dry December. There have been a few cold days and several days of snow. But there has also been a lot of blue sky and rather persistent temperatures in the single digits. The rain that begins the day I depart on Pacific Coastal continues every day until my return from California on January 5th, over two weeks later. After 17 consecutive days of rain, the locals have had enough. I arrive back in Powell River after a Christmas holiday of nearly constant fair, warm skies in Los Angeles. I am ready for some rain, while the locals are ready to be done with it.

A week later, the historic record of 32 days of rain, as recorded at Powell River Airport, looks like it may be broken. It has now rained for 24 consecutive days, and there is nothing in the weather forecast except precipitation, as far out into the northern Pacific as the weather satellites can see. One of the local radio headline stories proclaims that travel agency visits are up 23 percent for this time of the year. Arizona, California, and Mexico are the destinations of choice. I've gladly left the sun, but everyone here is dreaming of finding it.

On the 25th day of rain, there is an unexpected break. It's not enough to void progress (if you call it that) towards the 32-day rain record. But after an early morning shower (which counts towards the record), some blue sky appears. And the sunny patches grow.

On the telephone, John hems and haws. He doesn't believe what he sees. It's been too long since there was sunshine, and John doesn't trust the weather. Finally, as noon approaches, he agrees to try a quad ride. I am convinced the weather will hold. John is reluctant to trust the now mostly sunny skies. In any case, it will need to be a brief ride, since sunset comes early this time of year.

* * * * *

We off-load our quads at Mud Lake. John and Bro lead Margy and me north to the Granite Lake turnoff. Bro, dressed in his blue raincoat, sniffs at the sky as if he doesn't trust the conditions either.

There is a spur off the road to Granite Lake which caught John's attention on a previous ride. He knows it goes as far as Sweetwater Creek, the outlet from Granite Lake. What lies beyond is unknown. The trail is a deactivated logging road, and it should be relatively easy to rejuvenate. The old road crosses flat terrain that leads towards the creek. Beyond the creek, if we can get across, the topography slopes uphill.

Soon we reach the turnoff to the old logging road. I would not have even noticed it, but John marked it on his previous visit with a strand of fluorescent pink trail marking tape.

When we pull off the Granite Lake road, we face a short stretch of bushwhacking. The trail tracks through alders and bushes that John has already partially trimmed back. Then the old logging road opens into a lush forest with a clear path to follow. Healthy-looking small trees speckle the landscape on all sides.

"Birch trees?" I ask. It is not a common tree here, but this bark has broad dark mottled strokes on gray, and it looks like birch to me.

"No, they're alders," replies John.

"I'm used to alders being small, ugly trees near roads," I observe. "These trees are beautiful, and look how big the trunks are."

"They're usually stunted and crowded into areas near the roads, but these have lots of space to grow," says John.

"Are they good for lumber?" I ask.

"Furniture, but only when they're young. Good for firewood too."

Many of these trees are young and healthy. A few older alders, rotted inside, have tumbled over the trail. This requires us to stop every 100 feet or so, to clear away fallen trunks and branches. Otherwise, this trail would be nearly impassible for our quads. Of course, John has already been all the way to the creek, by himself, on his previous visit. These trees have fallen since then. Trails change quickly.

Every few minutes, John stops and cranks up his chainsaw. I hop off my quad to assist with clearing the saw's aftermath from the trail. We make good progress. The skies cooperate too. Bright blue pierces through the forest canopy.

In one broad opening in the trees, only scattered alders dot the landscape. A trail sign, in amazingly good condition, is nailed to a tree: "Plantation Road." It does have the feel of a plantation, the type you might find in an artificially cultivated area. But this isn't Virginia.

After several miles of stop-and-go to clear the trail with the chainsaw, we reach the end of the drivable stretch. The forest thickens against the bank of Sweetwater Creek, with its water tumbling down from Granite Lake. To our left is a jumble of giant logs, one with thick old cable extending along its span. The old logging road crossed the creek here, and the bridge must have been a massive structure. Today the creek runs through a series of rapids where the bridge originally stood, but there is a spot where we can get across. Fallen trees have created a temporary span of the creek, and I am able to crawl across the slippery moss-covered logs. This would be no place to fall into the cold rapids below.

John finds a spot to cross farther upstream. Bro probably won't be able to straddle the jumbled logs, and it would be disastrous if he fell into the rushing water. The spot is wide, but less than a foot deep. John ably hops across, stepping on protruding large rocks to prevent water from flowing over the top of his waterproof boots. On the other side, he tries to entice a reluctant Bro to take the cold plunge. After considerable barking and hesitation, Bro finally scampers across. He isn't very brave when it comes to raging creeks, but he isn't going to let John continue the hike without him,

Margy makes it over the tangled logs to join us, and now we are free to see where the trail on this side leads. It's not much of a trail, and it doesn't look like anyone has walked it in months, maybe years.

"I'm not sure where this goes," says John. "It's been a long time since I've been on a trail I've never hiked."

There is a hint of excitement in his voice. John has been everywhere in this region. Make that almost everywhere.

"Could you make a bridge across the creek for quads?" I ask. It looks impossible, but I know he, his brothers, and the ATV Club have accomplished some amazing trail renovations.

"Not a problem," John replies. "It looks tough, but we'd just need to groom the approach on both sides of the creek, dig out a few boulders and roots, and we'd be across. Our quads could handle that spot I crossed without a bridge, if the approaches are cleared."

"It looks like this trail goes quite a ways on this side," I say. "So I guess a bridge would be worth the effort."

"The ATV Club would be glad to help," John continues. "But there's no use even considering it unless this trail goes somewhere. It might just end in an old slash, but I'm hoping it takes us up to a good viewpoint. Then it would be worth building a way across."

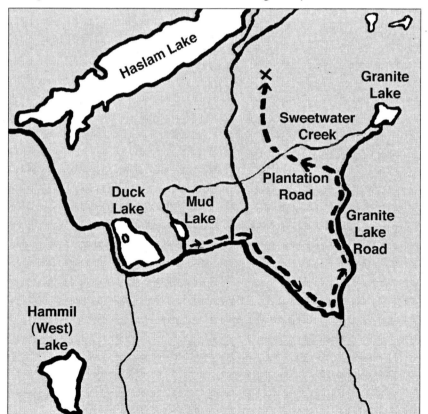

As we continue along the less-than-obvious trail, we parallel the creek. Then we split away from it, encountering a series of small brooks that are easy to step across. Margy is lagging behind, but John and I wait at most of the turns on the nebulous trail to make sure she is still on the path behind us. After several such stops, it seems obvious Margy is having no trouble following the trail, but she is hiking a lot slower than us.

On this side of the creek, the path is not nearly as evident. In fact, following John, I notice he turns at spots where I might have continued straight ahead. The going isn't tough, but the trail is far from distinct. At one point, I'm sure the trail angles off to the left, but John turns right.

"I thought that was the trail," I admit, motioning behind us to the left.

"No, take a look at the gap in the trees up ahead. You can see the trail passes through there, so you need to keep looking ahead for clues."

We are soon climbing directly uphill in increasingly steep terrain. We cross another small creek and pant our way up a rocky portion of the trail. We hang onto adjacent branches to support our climb.

"Better wait for Margy to catch up," says John.

It has been several minutes since we checked her progress behind us. So we wait. And we wait.

"Maybe she turned at that spot that confused me," I say.

John yells for Margy, and I try to follow suit, but my yell is not nearly as robust as his. John whistles too, a rousing and shrill sound that causes Bro to jump in his tracks. We hear nothing in reply. We can see several hundred feet below us on the trail. There is no Margy.

"Better head back down," says John. He sounds worried. And that worries me.

As we start down the trail, John and I continue to yell for Margy, to no avail. Finally, after a few hundred meters, we hear Margy yelling "Hello?!" below us. Then we see her coming out of the woods, well off the trail and below us to our right.

"I guess you're lost," says Margy.

"Yeah, right," replies John.

She is soaked from her waist down. She slowly clambers back onto the trail next to us.

"Not only did I get off the trail," she explains, "I also managed to fall into one of those little creeks. I'm soaked."

But Margy is still in great spirits and insists on continuing up the trail with us. So we reverse course again and start upward. When it gets even steeper, I decide it is time to rest and let John continue without me. Margy elects to go with John, but I use my standard author's excuse:

"Need to take some notes," I say, as I pull out my small spiral notebook that accompanies me everywhere. "Maybe I should document Margy's adventure into the forest."

"You could get really lost around here," says John. Then he and Margy continue up the slope without me. When they are out of sight, I relax under a tree with a natural log bench at its base. I put my notebook away, lean back against the tree, and enjoy a lazy 15-minute break. An author's excuse works every time.

* * * * *

Three days later, on Sunday, there is another temporary break in the weather. A predawn shower adds an additional day towards the rainfall record. It is now only 4 days to break the historic run of 32 days. But tomorrow's forecast for "further clearing" indicates the outcome of the rain record is now in doubt.

The latest weather implies two things – uncertainty that we'll hit 32 days; and serendipity for the Powell River ATV Club. The club has scheduled its New Year's Ride for today. But the persistent rain, until now, has provided little hope of the event coming off as scheduled. Yet, the day dawns sunny and mild. It's gonna work after all.

* * * * *

We pull off Highway 101 near the Wildwood gas station. Waiting beside the road are three pickups with quads in their beds and a compact car towing a quad trailer. Poki has offered to lead those of us who don't know where Pete and Lynn live. Their home near Lund will be the launching point for the ATV Club's group ride. Club members stand around in the gas station, drinking coffee and chewing the fat.

I've never been on a large group ride, and I'm a bit apprehensive. Will it proceed at a snail's pace, as riders in the group get spread out and then have to catch up? Will it be lacking in challenge, since the ATV Club's group ride policy is to ride to the level of the most inexperienced rider and the lowest-powered bike?

Margy has different concerns. She is nervous about having to park our quad trailer in a congested area. She is also concerned about being able to keep up with the group on her two-wheel drive quad. What if she is in the middle of the pack during a hair-raising precipitous climb? It's not like pulling over to the side of the trail, as she does when she is with John and me.

At the Wildwood stop, I explain to Poki that Margy needs lots of room to swing the trailer because she doesn't like backing up.

"No problem," says Poki as he sips his coffee from a paper cup. "I'll take care of it. Pete's place is huge, so we'll find you a roomy spot to off-load."

"She'd prefer a half-mile turn radius," I banter. Margy gives me a stare, while Poki grunts out one of his classic choking laughs.

Two more pickups arrive, and then Poki says: "It's time." Everyone goes to their truck (and one compact car). The vehicles pull out onto the highway in near-unison. Our truck is parked the farthest down the road in a wide turnoff, so Margy is just starting her truck as everyone else pulls by. I notice Poki is next to last in line. I guess everyone knows how to get to Pete's house – they just wanted to meet at the gas station for coffee.

Pete and Lynn live on a 30-acre spread near Lund, with their dirt driveway running off the west side of the highway. We wind down the driveway past another house before reaching the spacious parking area. Poki is right – this place can hold a lot of trucks and quad trailers. As we roll in, at least 10 pickups are already parked and off-loading their quads.

Margy comes to a temporary halt to survey the situation. Poki immediately jumps out in front of her, pointing towards a grove of trees straight ahead.

"It's wide open over there!" He shouts to be heard over the sound of the other vehicles. "Park right up next to the trees, anywhere you like."

I glance at Margy and perceive a sign of relief in her face. It's the perfect off-load spot for a two-quad trailer.

As we pull into the spot, trucks continue to roll into the parking area that straddles the wide space between the house and workshop. An old flatbed truck rattles in with three quads aboard.

Pete and Lynn walk around, greeting everyone and reminding us the ride will begin as close to 10 o'clock as we can manage. But there are lots of vehicles arriving at the last minute, so they don't want to start until everyone has a chance to get their quads ready. A few anxious riders crank up their bikes and zip around the parking area.

Two of John's brothers, Rick and Dave, off-load their quads. Mario is here. So are Tony, Dan, Jack, and a lot of other riders I've previously met. There are plenty of new faces too. Quads now zoom around every which way. The kids are getting restless.

"Line 'em up!" yells Pete. He thrusts an arm towards the direction we entered the driveway. I notice the gate has been swung closed. It's a hint we will peel off the parking area before we reach the driveway. There is a trailhead to the left. Pete has assigned a rider to park his quad next to the gate, so there is no doubt where we should turn.

Twenty-six quads rev their engines and begin to line up single-file, some crowding in from the sides. The line narrows as quads pull forward. I pick a spot about mid-way in the line and wave Margy in front of me.

We enter the trail near the driveway gate and wind through Pete's acreage. Then we cross Highway 101. For a brief few moments, 26 off-road vehicles hit paved road and are technically illegal vehicles on a highway. But it is pretty much a straight shot across the pavement, and we handle it carefully. The RCMP could make a bundle on us today, but I doubt they would bother such an orderly procession.

We wind along an uphill gravel (then dirt) road towards the south end of Okeover Inlet. I've looked on a map, and there is no published road or trail to take us across the south end of Okeover to Southview Road. In reality, there are several unmarked trails that accomplish this goal. We head towards one of them.

We are already getting strung out, but close enough together that I can see at least a dozen quads in front of me. Directly in front of me is Margy, and in front of her is the first problem. The problem quad begins to spew tools, ropes, and an assortment of straps from its aft rack. The trail is narrow here, so everyone from Margy on back comes to a screeching halt.

The quad has dropped its metal storage basket and its contents onto the trail. Several riders rush forward to assist. It takes awhile to gather the stuff and restrap it to the quad. While the rider reattaches equipment to his rear rack, the quad behind me pulls out of line and inches past us. I wave for Margy to follow, and then the rest of us slip past the problematic quad. Our riding group is now split into two segments. We are at least 5 minutes behind the first group, unless they have stopped to wait for us.

The leader of our subgroup zooms ahead in an attempt to catch the rest of the riders. Soon he has outdistanced Margy to the point where he is no longer visible. Effectively, Margy is in the lead of our group now. I know Margy, and I know she is not happy with this.

As we approach a split in the trail, I watch Margy slow and edge toward the trail to the right. She stops, and four quads instantly appear in my rearview mirror. As we come to a stop, Margy yells to me: "Tracks!"

She's right. There are fresh quad tracks to the right, so that must be the way everyone has gone. But there's still that uncertain feeling, and I'm sure it is within Margy too. I motion to the right with my arm, and Margy starts down the short slope that marks the beginning of the new trail. She proceeds tentatively at first, and then starts to accelerate. At the first upslope, Margy slows to survey its narrow rutted surface and accelerates a bit too late. She comes to a halt against a large tree root. Margy is now wedged between the tree and a deep rut. She spins her two-wheel drive tires, but her quad doesn't move. Everyone comes to a halt behind her.

I watch Margy back her quad the best she can within the confined area. She thrusts forward again. It ain't gonna work.

I hop off my quad and run forward to give her a push. It doesn't take much – Margy's bike is light. I am able to capitalize, as her rear wheels spin and spin, then briefly catch on the root. As I push from behind, she's up and over the rough spot. We are on our way again.

The trail winds across the south tip of Okeover Inlet for about a kilometer. Then it dumps out onto Southview Road. Pete and Lynn are waiting at the intersection, Lynn doubling behind Pete on their big Honda. Their small black dog is squeezed between them. I pull up behind Margy, who has stopped next to them.

"Everybody's got to learn to wait at each intersection!" Pete yells over the sound of our engines. "If they don't, they'll lose the riders behind them." He's preaching to the choir.

"A quad lost its rear cargo box on a narrow section back there," I explain.

Pete nods in understanding. I don't mention we were delayed a few more minutes by Margy's stuck quad. We wait at the intersection for the rest of our group to catch up.

"I didn't like that very much," Margy says to me.

"I know," I reply. She doesn't have to explain any further.

We're off again, and within a few miles we catch up with the rest of the group. They are waiting for us at the Okeover stop sign that juts up in the middle of nowhere. As we pull up behind these quads, it's an amazing sight. There are 15 quads at the intersection, and behind me I see the headlights of another 10. We all crowd together in an impressive gathering of quads on a small slice of dirt road.

After a few minutes, we are on our way again, climbing to cross eastward along the Theodosia Forest Service Road towards Appleton

Creek. At the bridge over the creek, we encounter a light dusting of newly fallen snow. The full snow pack appears suddenly only a short distance up the road. Within a half-kilometer segment, the landscape goes from green and brown to totally white.

We start up into the Bunster Range. The snow is now almost a foot deep, and the lead quad faces quite a challenge, even with four-wheel drive. When you're first through the snow, you face an absolute limit of about a foot of snow. In our position, halfway back within the convoy, it's a simpler matter. We put our tires in the snow tracks ahead of us, take advantage of the worn down center hump, and press on.

Then we reach the final steep hill that leads over the Bunsters. We stop at the base of the hill. Margy turns around and gestures to me apprehensively.

"We can turn around here," I yell over the sound of our engines. "I don't think they are going to get much farther up that hill anyway." Margy looks relieved.

Before we can pull off to the side of the trail and begin maneuvering to reverse our course, a quad near the lead turns around and heads down towards us. Now everyone is trying to turn around, but it isn't easy to get our bikes out of the deep grooves we've cut in the snow. It's a struggle, but we help each other by pushing and rocking quads until we are all headed back down the hill.

After a lunch break and an impromptu campfire near the Appleton Creek Bridge, our group splits. Margy and I elect to stay with the main contingent, which will follow the trail southward to Sliammon Lake. Then we'll wind down Wilde Road to an unmarked trail that parallels Highway 101 and back to our starting point. Another smaller group elects to enter Theodosia Valley, a more challenging route. They'll encounter overflowing streams that create temporary lakes in the landscape. These quads will then backtrack to meet us at Pete and Lynn's house.

For Margy and me, it's a 54-kilometer ride during a few precious hours of sunny breaks. The next day, rain reappears for the 29th consecutive day. The record towards 32 days of non-stop precipitation is still alive.

Chapter 9

Biking Van Anda

After a trip to the States, I arrive in Powell River in late November to find several inches of snow on the ground. It's confined to the higher locations in Westview, with its added few hundred feet of elevation. Joyce Avenue defines a dividing line between rain and snow. The airport (425 feet above sea level) has snow banks left from the previous few days, but the lower part of town shows little evidence of the storm.

After a night at our condo, Margy and I plan to go up the lake the next day. But the morning dawns with puffy cumulus clouds against a bright blue sky. This time of year, I find it important to grasp every non-rainy day as an opportunity to get outside on the trails or the chuck. This day is too good to leave behind, although it would be fun to enjoy some sun at our float cabin.

A phone call to John results in a surprise – he isn't interested in going riding. John has had enough of the cold for a while. Instead, he plans to head up the lake to Cabin Number 1. I visualize him huddled in his jacket on the cabin deck, kicked back in his white plastic lounge chair, absorbing the sun's warm rays.

As an alternate plan, the Bayliner needs exercise. It will be an opportunity to wash off the salt-water critters growing on the hull and especially the stern drive's leg. The chuck is seductively calm. Texada Island is a reasonable destination, with our bikes aboard for some exercise.

Surprise – the Bayliner's front deck is covered with a light layer of snow. This barely-cold-enough sea level marina allowed snow to accumulate during the recent storm. Maybe the rock breakwater formed a cold pocket. I carefully remove the tarp over the command bridge to prevent damaging the frozen Naugahyde. I gently fold the tarp over on itself and place it under the instrument panel, to let it warm and dry.

Ten pumps of the throttle before starting may be too much, but I've learned the cold engine needs lots of priming. The starter spins nicely, and the motor sputters briefly. But it refuses to run. I turn off the key and try two additional shots of throttle. The engine starts, runs smoothly for a few seconds, and dies again. But on the next unprimed attempt, it roars to life with vigor. I set the throttle just above idle to allow the motor to warm up slowly.

* * * * *

Margy and I ease out of the breakwater, poking our way into Malaspina Strait, separating Powell River from Texada Island. We are perched on the command bridge, wrapped in our winter jackets and gloves. This morning, the channel is packed with commercial activity. The Comox ferry is pushing its way out of the dock, and a variety of tugs and barges are headed up and down the strait. Between the Bayliner and Texada is a seemingly jammed mass of boats.

A tug tows a boom of logs south on a lengthy tether. Another tug, towing two huge containers, is chugging north. Getting between a tug and its load is a scary thought. But the ferry knows how to navigate through these obstacles, so I decide to follow.

We cross the *Queen of Burnaby's* developing wake, as it turns to pass between the north end of Texada and Rebecca Rock. We accelerate and come up on-plane at 15 knots, slowly catching the ferryboat, which is not yet up to cruising speed.

Once clear of the two tugs and their loads, I turn left and angle across the ferry's wake once again. They are significant swells now, but fun to challenge in the otherwise calm sea. On the other side of the disturbed water, there are no more obstacles. We cross smoothly to Texada, aiming in the general direction of the hidden (to us) harbour of Van Anda.

We aren't as fully prepared for navigation today as normal, but it is only a short voyage. The portable GPS is in our cabin up the lake, and even the harbour diagrams are not in the Bayliner today. I slow a bit, turn to angle towards the island's shoreline, and give the helm to Margy. I go downstairs to look for some old-fashioned navigation charts.

I find a basic boating guide next to the charts, but I can't find any references to Van Anda. I check the guidebook's index again. Even though the coverage includes this region, neither "Texada" nor the local alternative spelling of "Vananda" are listed. Texada Island is obviously not for recreational boaters.

Back upstairs on the command bridge, I try to fold the chart to a reasonable size. With GPS, I tend to forget the challenges of hardcopy charts. In fact, little navigation assistance is really needed today. We intercept Texada's shoreline well north of Van Anda, and then follow it southward.

Although Van Anda's harbour is hidden until on top of it, we are using landfall navigation to assure we don't miss it. It's similar to purposeful off-course dead reckoning in an airplane, where you intercept a highway well before your destination. Then you fly along the road to your target airport. It's a lot safer than trying to fly directly to an airfield, missing by a little, and erroneously turning the wrong way along the highway. When fuel is critical (especially in airplanes), it's a safer though less-direct route.

Once we get within a kilometer of Van Anda, it is easy to identify. We slip past the red navigation marker (red-right-returning) and pick a docking spot at the outermost finger. Compared to my previous visit here in June, the docks are nearly empty.

As we off-load our bicycles from the boat, the sound of a low flying airplane draws close. The noise permeates the air, echoing within the harbour. As the aircraft comes closer, the engine's roar is obviously that of a powerful turboprop, most likely a seaplane. The sound approaches from just outside the breakwater, the airplane still blocked from our view by the line of stacked rocks. Then the roar dissipates as the aircraft reduces power and lands (better be a seaplane!). From around the corner of the jetty, a Cessna Caravan on floats taxis in. The seaplane looks brand new in its shiny blue and white paint.

The Caravan is pointed directly towards us, and I worry that we have taken his docking spot. But I know from my previous visit that this dock is normally full of boats right to the tip. There is a lot of end-space for the floatplane on the next dock.

The Cessna angles towards the adjacent finger, cuts its engine when about 50 feet away, and glides perfectly into place against the dock. This airplane is the largest single-engine floatplane manufactured today. The powerful 675-shaft-horsepower turboprop can carry up to twelve people. The airframe is huge. The fuselage sits up high above the water on an intricately braced float structure. Six windows along each side and a big three-bladed prop make the brawny seaplane look massive compared to my Piper Arrow.

The pilot steps out and down to the dock to secure his lines. A family of four follows him, including two young children. I wonder if these youngsters know what a unique event they have just experienced. They probably consider it just a part of their routine life. With my 7000 hours of flying experience, I have been inside a floatplane only once, and it was not in an environment nearly as sublime as this.

The pilot wears a white shirt and tie, not the mark of a member of this family. He is clearly a charter pilot, commanding a pristine turboprop on floats, a valuable piece of aviation equipment. If it is nearly new, the value hovers near a million dollars. The middle-aged pilot is certainly highly experienced, based on his perfect docking, the most difficult aspect of floatplane operation. Like the oblivious youngsters, I wonder if he knows what a unique aviation life he is experiencing. This pilot isn't making big bucks hauling passengers on an airliner from Vancouver to Toronto, but his daily adventures in the sky are to be envied by the most senior airline captain.

* * * * *

I have warned Margy that the docks here are deteriorated, narrow, and wobbly. I remember them distinctly from my earlier visit. But we find the outer dock constructed of new wood, solid and visibly attractive. In fact, as we walk our bikes to the shore, all of the dock sections are like-new.

The unmanned Van Anda Boat Club office lives up to the reputation of the old wharf. It is a dilapidated shack with a faded sign proclaiming: "Day Parking $2." There is no one to pay. Margy looks around the other side of the shack for an honor box, but there is none.

We stop at the marina's entrance to check the air in our bicycle tires. Here I offer Margy some advice from my previous visit on-foot:

"It gets hilly fast, so let's stay in the lower section. There's probably not much to see, but it beats the hills we'll find if we go very far up the road."

"Sure," she replies. "I'm all for avoiding hills."

"I bet every house around here has a barking dog," I predict, "so be ready to defend yourself. If a dog starts to chase your bike, keep your foot cocked back. Be ready to give him a quick kick in the chops. It's your best defense."

I'm just full of helpful advice.

"Unless, of course, that totally pisses him off," she notes.

True, it's a gut call that a bicyclist has to make when the situation arises. But I visualize a lot of barking dogs here and not many bicycles to chase.

As we climb up the road from the dock, the first few hundred feet from the harbour are steep. So our biking adventure begins with walking our bikes. We trudge past an industrial salvage yard, where a skip-loader pushes bulky rusting treasures around. Then the climb ends, and we hop onto our bikes.

The road splits, and I lead us to the left on the smaller spur. This road seems to take us towards a residential area. There is a brief uphill stretch that we pedal up fairly easily. Then the street levels among a group of houses, each of its own unique design. They are wooden structures of different colors and shapes, all small and a nice change from imposing city homes.

A young boy appears ahead of us, walking with a dog. I just knew it! The youngster and his dog peel off to the right side of the road before we reach them. They climb the porch steps of a small house that sits only a few meters of the street. As the boy opens the unlocked door, the dog clambers ahead of him into the house. It's our first dog, a non-problem. It is also the last dog we see today. As for barking, there is none.

We ride past more small houses with cluttered yards. Around the corner lies a school, with only three vehicles in the large roadside parking lot. Playground equipment is scattered in the adjacent schoolyard. It has the look of an elementary school. But where is everybody on this weekday in late November?

From here the road curves farther to the right and starts back downhill. We pass more petite houses, then turn left at an intersection, and pause at what looks like a drainage ditch that passes beneath the road. The small bridge has a roadside sign: "Trout and Salmon Creek." It looks like a nearly-dry ditch today, even though this is the rainy season.

Another hundred feet up the road is the general store, with one truck in the parking lot. Across the street from the store is the post office. There is little activity here, except for a man exiting the store and headed towards his truck. It's not much of a town, and that's part of its unique charm. We sit astride our bikes in front of the post office, in this pleasant center of nowhere.

From here, the climb quickly steepens, so we wisely reverse course. We cross the bridge again (no trout, no salmon) and turn left along the gravel road that parallels the creek. The road begins to climb, and I lead us over the first rise. When we encounter a bigger hill beyond, I do a U-turn.

"It's not much of a ride so far, but is it enough for today?" I ask Margy.

"It's fine," she replies.

I'm certain Margy is surprised that I'm on the verge of finishing one of our exploratory bicycle rides without overdoing it. Usually I have to go just a little farther, until the way back is exhausting.

On our return to the harbour, we get a bit lost (meaning: I think I know the general direction to the harbour). I try a street to the right.

Then another right. It leads us to the home where the boy and dog entered a half hour earlier. I stop in front of the house.

"See, I knew where we were," I brag.

"Right," Margy replies, in a tone that reminds me she sees through me.

It's enough for one day, although the ride has been brief. As we start down the final stretch of road to the docks, the hill is too steep to take at full speed unless I continue straight ahead onto the breakwater. So I avoid using my brakes and continue past the dock entrance and out onto the spit that shelters the bay. My downward momentum, coupled with the easy flat ride on the breakwater's dirt road, carries me nearly to the end without pedaling.

At the tip of the breakwater, a solitary straight-backed office chair sits in a turnout among the rocks. It has a tattered plastic-covered cushion for a seat and a metal-framed back support with the upholstery missing. I have a few minutes before Margy catches up (with her brakes on during the descent to the dock, I'm sure). I hop off my bike and take a position of command authority in the chair, overlooking the tip of the jetty. The seat is water-soaked, and I can feel moisture saturating my pants. But the view is awesome.

I sit at the tip of the Van Anda breakwater. To one side, I have a fine view of the boats in the harbour and the dominating Cessna Caravan on floats. On the other side is the Malaspina Strait. Across the open water, perched on the hilly shoreline, sits Westview with its marina at the shore. Farther north, the Powell River townsite and the tall smokestack of the paper mill provide an impressive scene.

Towering cumulus clouds catch the backlight of a late autumn sun riding ever lower in the west. To the south, down the strait towards Vancouver, the sky is dark, with rain showers thrusting downward from the clouds.

Here I sit at the end of a breakwater near a tiny town on a nearly uninhabited island. Maybe the seaplane pilot and the family he brought to this tranquil island today don't recognize the value of this spot. But I recognize this place in time and space for what it is worth. And, to me, it's worth millions.

◊ ◊ ◊ ◊ ◊ ◊

John and Bro ham it up on Mount Mahony

Margy on firewood patrol in Hole in the Wall

Olsen's Landing on Powell Lake, from Piper Arrow

On Beartooth Main, looking south

Motorcycles on Bayliner, near Goat River

John and Bro on E-Branch trail near Alpha Lake

John and Margy at Quad Lookout on Blue Ridge

Winter snow levels at Hole in the Wall seldom exceed an inch

John and Bro on J-Branch trail near Murphy Lake

Margy at Gibson's Beach, with Harwood Island in background

Low clouds flow through First Narrows near Cabin Number. 3

Rick and John with Bro, overlooking Lancelot Inlet

John and Bro on Blue Ridge, looking down on Haslam Lake

Seaplane and Campion at Cabin Number 3, Hole in the Wall

Bro relaxes in the bow of the Campion

Margy, Bro, and John go beachcombing in Hole in the Wall

Chapter 10

Goat 1

In the final months of preparation for publication, *Up the Main* faced a unique challenge. The book was nearly complete, but the cover photo still not selected. It's something that's usually automatic, as it was with *Up the Lake's* cover photo of the double rainbow from Hole in the Wall or this book's photo of winter hiking on Heather Main.

In my mind, the cover for *Up the Main* required a stunning photo of the region's geography. There could be no equipment (quads) in the photo to spoil the natural beauty. Supernatural scenery is readily available in the region, and my photo files are full of remarkable natural scenes. But book covers are well known for remarkable scenery, and this cover must stand out from the rest. Nothing quite fit my requirements.

* * * * *

I stumble for ideas regarding a natural cover scene. My aspirations are plagued by washed out pictures, the result of high altitude lighting, less-than-perfect sky conditions, and an amateur at the shutter. But shoot enough photos and the right one appears. As in the rainbow cover for *Up the Lake*, you can't force it. Just give it time, and the photo will come to you.

But it doesn't come. The book is otherwise complete, so panic begins to set in. I ask John for assistance. He understands exactly what I want, and he takes me there.

It is a struggle up the remote trail near the Eldred River, above Goat Lake. The path, overgrown with alders, leads to a nondescript turnoff near an old logging slash. Then it's a short hike (thrash) to a lookout spot, visibly trampled as a viewpoint by the few visiting hikers who come this way. Framed on either side by forested slopes, majestic

Mount Alfred thrusts upward into the pale blue sky, its glaciated peak dazzling in the sun. It is the perfect photographic setting for the cover of a book.

"There's your photo," states John.

"Amazing," I remark. John has led me, without pause, to this photographic dream-site, smack dab in the middle of nowhere.

But we both know it isn't going to work. The sky is pale, and ashen clouds linger near the glaciers. The image will be washed out, regardless of our effort. Photos have their moment, and you can't force it. My memory of Mount Alfred, piercing up into the heavens that day, is imprinted in my brain, but it isn't on the cover of a book.

When I arrive back in town, I don't bother rushing to see what is in the camera. I know it is another instance of pale scenery – an insult to the grandeur of the region. Over time, I've learned that some scenes are not worth trying to capture in a photograph. They are best left inside the camera of my mind.

After the Mount Alfred picture expedition, I scan through my old photo files, determined to find a hidden gem. Several alternate covers are considered, and they are used in advance advertising for the book. None of these prospective photographs ever makes it to *Up the Main's* front cover. One image is nearly perfect in my mind's eye – a sky-reaching shot taken from Beartooth Main. But once again, the lighting isn't right, and this remarkable scene isn't properly captured.

I stoop to thievery. John's family has photo albums that depict the glory of the region. One night, I pour over photos with John's parents. An image of McVey Lake is perfect for the task, but its portrait-style perspective can't be properly harnessed for the cover of my book. Another particularly perfect photo is tempting, but I don't think a photo from Banff could be faked as representing Powell River.

* * * * *

"I've got the spot," says John, after Margy and I return from a brief trip to California. "But we'll need the perfect day."

The book is now completely ready to go except for the cover. But the right day doesn't arrive in time, even if John has the perfect spot. However, there is one morning that just might work. An early autumn cold front has dropped through the region, and clearing is forecast. What we will find in the high country is anyone's guess. It's not exactly winter, but snow will be falling on the mountains soon. If we're going to act, there can be no delay.

Margy backs her truck into the hangar, and stops near the quad trailer's tow hitch. John has renovated the trailer (again) during our visit to the States. The latest improvements include new trailer wiring and a set of built-in rear ramps for loading. John has adapted standard Canadian Tire load ramps for the task, cutting them to fit into hefty mounting brackets. This trailer is built to survive an avalanche.

Before we hit the road today, a few final adjustments will be necessary. The trailer's license plate is still in my backpack, kidnapped during my hasty retreat from Canada. The plate, which traveled to and from California by mistake, is a properly issued ICBC registration. But having it in my backpack could have been a problem when clearing Customs. I doubt any explanation would have been adequate for discovery of a Canadian license plate as part of my unclaimed border-crossing goods.

Now the seemingly simple task is to remove an old license plate from the trailer and install the new one. But removing a license plate that John has bolted into place can be a challenge. He installs things to last. I recently watched him tighten Margy's trailer towing ball onto its mount using a vise. Good luck to anyone who tries to remove it.

The bolts in the old license plate are about four inches long and stout enough to hold a refrigerator door. I finally extract them and fasten the new plate in place. All is well now, except for the final wiring connection. The quick-disconnect plug that pops into the truck's bumper socket is missing. I know it is somewhere in the truck, undoubtedly in a logical location that John has selected. But it isn't logical to me.

I try the glove compartment, the rear seat toolbox, and a variety of other likely spots. The most logical spot will have to await discovery until we meet John at his house. (It is the perfect storage location, as expected, right in the truck's door storage pocket. "Why didn't you look there?" asks John.)

I hook up the trailer safety chains (hefty) and insert the pintle hook (itself a work of John-art). Finally I'm ready to guide Margy out of the hangar. Without the quick-disconnect plug, there will be no trailer turn signals or brake lights. Margy will need to use hand signals during the trip downhill. I wonder if they still teach hand signals in driver training?

As we exit the hangar, a seaplane with a "For Sale" sign blocks the normal entry to the paved ramp. It's simple to get around the aircraft, but it won't be as easy with our Piper Arrow. The aviation economy has continually slumped in recent years, and the Arrow is the only airplane left in this hangar. Boats and RVs now dominate the building. Our airplane is isolated and forgotten, held hostage in the hangar by a for-sale seaplane. But, for now, the chunky Cessna on floats looks spiffy sitting in the middle of the hangar exit.

After meeting John at his house and finishing our electrical hookup, we take over the outer island at the local gas station. We guzzle a lot of fuel – John's pickup, his quad, Margy's truck, plus two more quads on the trailer. Gas prices have been soaring lately. It makes you notice how every aspect of life is affected by oil. Wilderness exploration is no exception.

We follow the road south of Haslam and Duck Lake, then north to the turnout near Mud Lake. It's a wide area that allows Margy to comfortably back her truck into position, and provides an easy off-load for our quads.

We hustle through the standard off-load procedures. I don't want to keep John, Mr. Let's-Get-Going, waiting. I unhook the trailer safety chains, the pintle hook, and...

Wait! – I'm going too fast again. I don't need to disconnect the trailer here. The trailer can stay hooked to the truck. Even the ramps can stay down after our off-load, since they are part of the trailer's structure. So I reconnect the safety chains and pintle hook. I hop onto my quad, open the choke, and start the engine. I'll allow it to warm up while we continue to unstrap the bikes. It starts on first crank, and the engine warms smoothly. Then it quits. The gas valve is still in the "Off" position.

Why do I screw up so often when preparing my quad for action? Answer: as a pilot, I've become dependent on checklists. Quads may not be as complicated as an airplane, but being led step-by-step to a goal is a comfortable habit. It also explains why I never go flying without a checklist.

Margy is ahead of me with her preparation, and John is way ahead of both of both. Finally, without further delay, we're out of the parking area. John and Bro ride first, followed by Margy, and then me. At the first logging slash, John pulls to the side of the road, and we pull up behind him.

"Elk," says John. "Do you see them?" He knows we miss a lot, compared to his always-in-tune eyes. Neither Margy nor I see the elk.

"Hop across the ditch for a better look," says John.

I quickly cross the drainage ditch and up onto the edge of the slash. Margy follows behind me, struggling to climb up the rough 4-foot slope. We stand next to each other, scanning the slash, and then it hits us.

The elk are right in front of us, only 100 meters away, but their tan coats blend perfectly with their surroundings. A large bull stands out prominently, his 8-point rack dominating the scene. Six other elk walk ever-so-slowly away from us. They are not frightened by our presence.

"They seem so tame," I say to John, who has crossed the ditch with Bro to join us. "It's not hunting season, is it?" I ask, remembering a recent radio announcement regarding the start of hunting season.

"Not for these guys," replies John. "At least not until the elk population gets back up to normal."

Roosevelt Elk are part of an ongoing relocation project on the Sunshine Coast. Elk were moved to Powell River by barge and truck in the mid 1990s. Government officials estimate this year's local elk population at 150, for a total of 600 on the entire Sunshine Coast. When you ride this area and talk to others about elk, the population seems to be substantially higher.

Bro is standing beside us. He is looking around, ignoring the elk. Surely, he sees them.

"Look at Bro," I say. "He doesn't even seem to care. That's not like him."

"He doesn't see them yet," replies John. "And he can't seem to smell them either, like he does bear."

Suddenly, Bro spots the elk and barks up a storm, but he's not yet into his bear howl. Now Bro wants to chase them.

"Get back here!" yells John. Bro is prowling the edge of the slash, looking for a clear route to the elk. John grabs Bro around the neck before the dog finds a path. Bro continues to bark. The big bull elk looks our way, and then returns to his slow gait across the clearing. The rest of the elk don't even give Bro a glance.

"They're not afraid of dogs," says John. "Even mountain lions won't attack a herd, although they might try to corner an injured elk or a young one that's been separated from the rest."

"What about bears?" I ask.

"Pretty much the same," says John. "I don't think bears will attack a herd like this. That big rack on the bull can do a lot of damage."

I inspect the bull closer. He looks so gentle, yet so dangerous. Bro is lucky he doesn't get his wish today. Chasing elk can be hazardous to your health, with the rack on a bull a mighty strong weapon.

Back on the road, we continue up the main along Haslam Lake, and then onto the short stretch of new road that connects to Fiddlehead Farm. We take a snack break at the only building that remains on the old farm. It is nothing but log beams, a mostly intact floor, and windowless walls. All else has been scavenged over the past few years.

Two years ago, I remember John making a half-effort to play the old piano in this cabin. At the time, the piano was only a partially preserved relic, and what came out of it could not be called music. But at least it looked like a piano. It is now gone, an example of the continued deterioration of this landmark farm.

Back on the road, we transition onto Rainbow Main. Margy takes to this road like a champ – more specifically, a patient nearly recovered from quad "altophobia." Margy slows a bit on the main, but it is nothing like her last hellish moments only four months ago here, when she slowed to a crawl out of sheer fright. We're all pleased, but John expects even more improvement, in anticipation of future destinations that will require climbs along trails with an even steeper drop-off.

At the east end of Rainbow Main, we merge onto Goat Main (officially Goat Lake Main). Then we make the next right turn onto Goat 1. The climb is immediate.

Alders begin to creep into our path, an indication this road has not been used for logging in many years. The going gets tough, particularly because of the mix of cross-trenches and the alder infestation. Occasionally, a section of road breaks into the open, and the ride is generally pleasant. Bro disagrees – as John leads the way, he snaps off protruding alder branches for us, but a few whip back and whack Bro as he rides in his aft box. He ducks most of them. The indignity of it all.

As the trail narrows more, the trenches are deeper but still navigable. No large vehicles have been through here in a long time, and it shows.

The scenery is terrific, and the weather is holding. Maybe this will be the day for a cover photo to jump out and grab us. I stop at several locations and take lots of pictures, hoping for the magic scene.

Finally, the rocky surface gets particularly nasty, and we all stop. It's obvious that Margy shouldn't continue further. It's not her quad altophobia, nor the roughness of the slope, nor the lack of four-wheel drive on her quad that stops us. It's a combination of all those things. This is a place in the trail where the level of difficulty increases. Margy is glad to take a break here beside a beautiful roadside waterfall, to wait for John and me to return.

John leads me up the narrow, steep trail. In this section of the old road, snow season stunts the alders into dwarf scrub-brushes. They no longer impede our progress.

The rocky, rutted climb is a challenge for me, but the result is never in doubt. Although logging vehicles have not used the road in a long time, this portion of the trail is in good condition. Denuded of alders, it provides sweeping vistas of the mountains around us.

I pause often for photos. Clouds are beginning to creep near the higher peaks, and the brilliance of the thinner air at this high altitude is starting to degrade the scattering of light. From the images I see in the camera's viewfinder, the problem is obvious. The scenery I see in the camera's window is spectacular, but the photos that result will be washed out today. It's a common disappointment when taking pictures at high altitudes.

At one photo stop, John notices several mountain goats on the cliffs to the north. They are moving down the mountain, and he tries to help me spot them. But, as is common, John's eyesight is so superior to mine that I see nothing.

"Look for movement," he says. "They are coming down the cliffs, and you should see the moving white dots."

I find a pair of small binoculars in my backpack. I extract them and try to locate the place on the cliff where John sees the goats. As I adjust the focus knob, I catch a glimpse of a white dot. It's not clearly identifiable as a goat, but I know that is what it is. By the time I focus the binoculars, the goat is gone.

"They've moved into some trees," says John. "I don't see them now, but they should come out soon."

We wait for the goats to move out of the trees, but after five minutes, they have not reappeared. I put away the binoculars, and we are on our way again. We're on the final portion of the Goat 1 climb, up to the area John figures we will find the ideal cover photo opportunity. That is, if the peak of Freda Mountain is clear.

As we climb higher, the rocks take on a pinkish-violet hue. Even the dirt road seems to be similarly colored. It must be my sunglasses, or could it be a sign of hypoxia? I remove my glasses, and the color remains. I ask John if he sees it. He tells me, with a suspicious look, that the colors have not changed.

John spots a meadow to our left at the base of a small peak.

"Wouldn't it be nice to hike to the top of that ridge someday?" he asks. I know the answer. His brain is always in motion.

"We would start over there and work our way towards that gully, and then up the towards the ridgeline."

"That'd be a lot of work," I reply.

"Rick and I could find a route. We'll have to come back here, and see if it can be done."

We stop again at the top of the road at John's predicted photo spot for the ideal cover picture. I take a few photos. But the resulting pictures will not be grand. Freda Mountain is shrouded in clouds, and the skyline is washed out in the camera's viewfinder. The view to the naked eye, however, is magnificent.

John is disappointed that we have come this far only to find my cover photo out of reach. I am thrilled to have found this spot, clouds and all.

"I'm not worried about missing the photo," I tell him. "We'll have to come back, so you can show me this place when Freda is clear."

"It is such a beautiful place." John's statement is simple and to the point.

We'll be back.

* * * * *

A few weeks later, I abandon the concept of a sterile scenic cover photograph without equipment in the picture. Instead, I select a picture taken the previous year at Olsen's Landing. The photo of quads in the foreground, with a background of snow-capped mountains, is completely unlike the scene I sought. But it serves wonderfully on the cover of *Up the Main*.

Chapter 11

Winter on the Command Bridge

Motoring down the lake on a rainy October morning, I recognize a problem that needs to be solved before winter. Unlike summer journeys, when it is merely a matter of hopping into the boat, cranking the engine, and unhooking the lines, a winter jaunt is more demanding. On days that are both cold and rainy (or snowy), it is an even bigger challenge. During such conditions, with the full canvas package installed, the boat develops instant fogged windows. The canvas is wet, and the interior humid and cold. Thus, the glass becomes opaque. Add some rain or snow, and visibility is an even bigger problem.

This morning, I drive through the North Sea, the open water south of First Narrows that has been appropriately named by John. It's an area of converging winds, with flotsam hidden in the troughs. The rain is coming down hard, and my windshield wiper is trying to keep up. But the moisture on the inside of the window is a separate problem. Even my trusty little electrical defroster, plugged into the DC socket, is unable to clear the windshield. The heater has created a small hole to look through at an awkwardly low spot on the windshield. I drive hunched over, peering through this portal, seemingly oblivious to my surroundings.

In reality, I am not ignoring the background situation, and that's what bothers me the most. The side windows are totally fogged. If another boat is converging from the side, I'll likely not see it until it is on top of me (not literally, I hope). If a log pops out anywhere other than through my tiny defrosted portal, I'm doomed. This isn't the log-laden season for this lake, but the water is starting to rise with the autumn rains, and soon there will be flotsam everywhere. Logs from last summer sit on the shoreline, ready to be launched as floating wooden mines, waiting for the Campion to hit the trip wire.

As I pass John's Cabin Number 1 on the east shore, it dawns on me: this is totally unacceptable. The winter has not yet begun, and I am already driving without adequate forward visibility. What happens when the temperature drops further? How long before my luck with tunnel-vision runs out? Worse yet, beside me sits Margy, unable to render assistance, as she stares at the fogged window in front of her. Occasionally, she wipes the moisture away, just in time to see the biggest of the log mines and some of the converging boats. It is at times like this that a brain in motion is a disturbing thing – I realize other boats (blessedly few this time of year) are chugging up and down this lake in exactly the same situation. I can't see them, and they can't see me. Ignorance is bliss. Sometimes.

As we pass abeam Haywire Bay, I make up my mind. It's time to do something about this problem before it's too late. Our boat is a stern-drive, so there is an automobile-like engine sitting at my disposal just eight feet to the rear. Automobiles have defrosters, and so can boats. But this is a summer boat. And anything designed to solve this fogging problem will be a major modification.

John is the master of after-market mods. He visits the local boat shop and picks their brains. He learns about radiator kits and how they mate (or more accurately, don't mate) with water-cooled engines. Among the advice he receives regarding this raw-water system: "Tell the American to buy a new boat."

John doesn't give up. He designs (with blueprints only in his mind, of course) an air recirculation system. It's based on a modified bilge blower mounted near the windshield. The driver's window requires recirculated air as much as it needs heat; even cool airflow will help. Coupled with an added windshield wiper for the passenger side of the boat, this design might solve the problem, even without heat. Call it an ambient air defroster.

* * * * *

I surprise John by catching up to him at Pete's Plumbing, where he is scouring the shelves for tubing connectors. He acts shocked to see me here. I tell him I can find him anywhere in town, any time I desire. This is, of course, an innate trait he alone possesses, and we both know it. In reality, I phoned John's home a few minutes ago to learn of his whereabouts from Rick.

"Look at this," he says, holding a large black flange against a white plastic elbow. "This will go into the cup holder opening in the dash, and then I can bolt the whole thing down. It'll have a rotatable tube to duct the air wherever you want. In fact, it should blow the air all the way across to the passenger window."

"I like it," I reply. "But are you sure that flange will fit into the cup holder?"

"Should," is his reply. "Didn't measure it, but it looks right." John's eye has a built-in tape measure, accurate to a few sixteenths of an inch.

The salesman in the pipe section of the store is into the project now, spending his time discussing the design with John and offering alternative suggestions. We jump from shelf to shelf, comparing elbows and step-down connectors. Meanwhile, customers with more expensive projects in mind await the salesman's attention. Adapting plumbing tubing to a boat blower is far more interesting than discussing a major bathroom renovation.

John finally selects the flange he wants, and we walk to the cash register. I notice this is the plastic piece John pointed out to me the moment I entered the store, fifteen minutes ago.

"He's gonna do it his own way," the salesman says to me.

"I could have told you that," I remark.

The end product is a work of art, or more appropriately a classic John-design. The blower is mounted nicely out-of-sight below the dashboard, pumping a hefty blast through the cup holder onto the windshield. The new windshield wiper, installed on the passenger side, requires careful parking after each use. Otherwise, the hinged center windshield panel could crush the wiper when the window is opened.

"This boat wasn't designed for a wiper on the passenger side," says John. Of course, this boat wasn't built with a bilge blower cold-air defroster either. But, as usual, that doesn't stop John.

On the next rainy morning departure from the float, I crank up the engine, flick the windshield blower switch, plug in the DC heater, activate the wipers on both diver and passenger sides, and glide away from the cabin dock. During my trip down the lake, the view is seen through satisfyingly clear windshields.

* * * * *

Snowflakes lick the mossy ledge of the cliff, 50 feet above the waterline, as I gaze outward from the deck of my cabin. There is snow above, with wet slush falling on the deck. As the morning progresses, the day grows colder rather than warmer. The forecast calls for snow. A grey metallic sky agrees.

I've planned a run to town in the Bayliner. It's a chance to exercise the engine after a month of docked inactivity behind the cabin in the ocean boat's temporary winter home. The air is calm, and conditions are perfect, except for the snow. If it gets too cold, I can drive from inside the Bayliner. But the command bridge is where I want to be. The view from up-top is much better, and maneuverability is a lot easier with the improved visibility. The boat feels like a tug from down below and like a sport cruiser from above.

It takes awhile to get organized. Besides the packing up that is always required, this is the first voyage of the Bayliner during the winter. This boat is normally docked at the Westview Marina. Here on the lake, the ocean barnacles are being cleaned off the hull by the lake's freshwater wash-and-rinse. While docked at the cabin, this boat serves as an alternate source of transportation. To me, the 24-foot Bayliner is a big boat. Compared to the Campion, it is.

I layer my clothing and add a full-face ski mask and heavy gloves. The snow level has now reached the surface of the lake. It's not a heavy snowfall, but a soft dusting that scatters the diffuse sunlight as it falls. The Hole glitters in December splendor.

As I step aboard from the dock at the rear of the cabin, the boat creaks in the cold. Every step makes a crisp squeak under my wool-lined boots. The boat's aft deck is already covered with snow, deep enough to show my footprints in the virgin white. I consciously twist my feet as I walk in the snow, an enhanced squeaking effect that leaves giant footprints.

I raise the engine cover and check the oil. It is thick but clear and to the "Full" line. I move the battery switch from "Off" to "Both," take one last glance around the engine compartment (almost no bilge water), and close the cover.

I decide to start the engine from inside the boat's cabin, since it is warmer than the command bridge. But this is not where I will drive. For now, the tarp on the command bridge remains secured. In case the engine doesn't start, a strong possibility after this period of cold in-activity, I can quickly move over to the Campion for the trip to town.

Since the command bridge of the Bayliner requires considerable preparation, including removal of the protective tarp, starting the engine from below is easier. Five shots of slow prime with the throttle, and the engine cranks strongly and starts almost immediately. I am both surprised and pleased. The throttle remains slightly above idle for initial warm-up, and after a few minutes I am able to reduce power without stalling. During this brief interlude, I recognize my mistake.

Having started the engine from inside the boat, this is where it will have to be restarted if it stalls during the trip to town. With the engine running, the key can't be removed and taken up to the command bridge. Of course, I could correct this situation right now by shutting down and restarting from above. Don't mess with good luck, I conclude, since my success with quick starts for this engine hasn't been good. However, if I drive from above and stall during docking at the Shinglemill, I'll regret my decision. I'll have to rush downstairs to restart the engine before impacting the dock. I take a chance, and decide to press on.

At least I'm smart enough to turn off the bilge blower while I'm downstairs, so it can be controlled from the command bridge. A few moments without the blower during my transition to the upper deck will be safe.

As I pass the galley on my way aft, I almost forget Mr. Seagull. It is important to squeeze the hanging rubber good-luck-charm before every voyage. It is also wise, upon safe arrival, to thank the bird by giving him another quick squeeze. I'm not superstitious about flying two miles above the earth at three times highway speed in a small metal container. But Mr. Seagull gets the mandatory squeeze as I pass. His squawk seems a bit higher-pitched in the cold air: "Squ-awh-awk!"

It takes a few minutes to remove the tarp from he command bridge. I carefully fold the cover without creasing it in the cold. Then it's back down to the dock to unfasten the lines, three ropes that are curved stiff at their attachments. It is slow work in my heavy, winter gloves.

I gently step aboard the boat, trying to minimize my push away from the dock. Then, I climb the stairs to the command bridge again, and cover the seat with a towel to prevent my nylon snowsuit from sticking to the cold Naugahyde. I settle into the seat and shift into reverse, slowly backing away from the dock. As I clear the underwater cable that tethers the float cabin to shore, I slide into neutral, just in case the heavy braided wire is closer to the surface than it appears.

Beyond the cable, I shift into forward for a short burst of power, return to neutral to cross the cable again, and then shift solidly into forward. The Bayliner slowly exits the confined area behind the floating cabin.

Once clear of the firewood float and breakwater, I push the throttle up a bit, navigating around the morning's accumulation of flotsam. At this increased speed, visibility is substantially reduced in the gently falling snow. I'd like to pop on my sunglasses to ease the glare, but I should have thought of that before donning my ski mask.

I motor out of the Hole at a speed slow enough to allow plenty of time to think. It is a bit too late to run through a mental checklist. I immediately identify two missing items – my portable GPS and the satellite phone. My cell phone will work after clearing Cassiar Island, but it is still an unacceptable mental lapse. Then I remember that my cell phone battery is nearly dead, awaiting recharging in town. Forgetting the GPS is even worse – what if visibility drops to zero in the snow? The embarrassing part is that two fully-functional GPS receivers sit idle on the cabin's kitchen table. One is for both aviation and nautical use and the other for hiking. Either would show the lake's shoreline. There's nothing like making a double (or is it triple?) error while packing, and these omissions involve safety. Of course, I could turn around now and go back. But I don't.

I enter First Narrows at 5 knots, testing the feel of this bigger (to me) boat. Then, as the Bayliner approaches the North Sea, I turn off the blower and push the throttle forward. The water is calm, so I should be able to make good time today. But as I accelerate, visibility immediately decreases. The snow crystals glitter everywhere, and the cold causes my eyes to tear. I must slow down to see even a few feet ahead. The snow is heavier now, and it is cold on the command bridge. Maybe driving from below is worth a try.

It is much warmer down below, but I don't like the restricted view. The windshield is frozen, and the wiper flicks only some of the ice free. Moisture has condensed and frozen on the inside of the glass. Wiping it with a rag only keeps it clear for a few moments. That's the real purpose of the electric fan, sitting poised for action. Until now, its only purpose has been to move summer air around during warm nights in the boat's cabin. Today, the airflow should help clear the inside of the window.

I turn the fan on, and it winds up to high speed (don't need that), so I reach forward to move the switch to the "Low" position. But my clunky glove sticks out a bit too far, and the cold plastic blades hit it at high speed. Pieces of cold, brittle plastic go flying everywhere. The fan's speed goes from high to supersonic. I hastily fumble to turn it off. Two smashed straw-like remnants of the blades protrude from the hub. One fan destroyed.

This isn't working well at all. I've never had much luck while driving this boat from inside, and today is not a good day to practice. No matter how cold it is on the command bridge, it is where I feel most comfortable. From up there, I can more easily see logs hidden in the troughs of waves. So up I go again.

The snow has slackened a bit in the last few minutes. Big soft flakes are falling all around me. I stick my tongue through my ski mask and catch a snowflake. I let a few flakes build up on my glove, and then flick them off with my other hand, testing them for wetness. The flakes are super-wet and crystalline-structured, and the air seems warmer now. Or maybe I'm just getting used to it. Regardless of weather, the command bridge is where I should be.

The sun breaks through, even while huge snowflakes are still falling. I push the throttle forward, get comfortably on-plane at 20 knots, and trim the bow. I settle in for a cold but smooth ride.

In the midst of a sun-shower of snow, a workboat appears off my left side, converging with me from behind. We mutually approach the narrow passage between Cassiar Island and the shore. I am through the passage first, and then I alter course to the right, to give the crew boat more clearance.

As the other boat accelerates past me, I wave from the command bridge. I can't see if the driver waves back, but I'm sure he has a few words to say to the loggers on board:

"There's a guy up on the command bridge of that Bayliner, in a snowstorm. Ain't that just like those stupid recreational boaters?"

If he knew I'm an American, he'd really have something to say.

By the time I am abreast of Cabin Number 1, the snowflakes are intermittent. They swirl around my head, caught by the airflow above the narrow, open windshield. Blue sky beckons to the south. I can see rays of light focused on the Shinglemill, several kilometers ahead. The view from the command bridge is fantastic. Snow-laden trees and patches of bright blue sky enhance the supernatural scene, as snowflakes churn around me.

Approaching the marina, I pull back on the throttle, push the two trim switches to full bow-down, and switch the bilge blower on. As I swing into the breakwater, I remember the ignition key downstairs. If I flameout now, I'm in trouble in this tightly confined space. One way to counteract the situation is to slow as far as possible, and this boat will decelerate to a crawl.

I creep slowly towards my parking spot, a docking space meant for the smaller Campion. I've docked here before with the Bayliner, but it is tricky. The neighboring boat in my two-boat slot is as big as his space allows, and there's a kicker on the transom – on the same side as my berth. Of course, today the kicker is tilted, prop-outward, towards my side of the dock. This will require precise timing for drift, with no flameout, please.

Big snowflakes continue to twirl around me, but now it is mostly clear above. I ease towards the dock finger, calculating the boat's drift in my head. John would make this look like child's play. I might make it look like a child terrorizing the neighborhood. The wind is light and from behind, so drift will be enhanced. I'll need to start my turn early.

I begin swinging the wheel to the right, and I feel the stern moving at just the right speed. If I barely clear the neighbor's kicker as I drift towards the dock, the Bayliner should slip right into the open berth. It's looking amazingly good, although the drift now seems a tad too fast. I shift into neutral to slow further.

The kicker slides by the right side of my bow, its prop only inches from my starboard gunnel. The Bayliner is now parallel to the dock and sliding towards it ever so slowly. The bow is about to hit the front railing, and the left side of the Bayliner is close to the dock. Both the bow and port side touch simultaneously and smoothly. There is no bounce. A perfect docking, and a perfect ending to an exhilarating trip.

The Bayliner stays firmly in position. There is no hurry to jump ashore, since this boat is precisely parked, hugging the dock. I stick out my tongue and catch one more snowflake. It tastes wonderful.

* * * * *

In the winter, the wood stove burns hot nearly 24-hours a day. In the middle of the night, I usually awaken and catch the dying coals before the fire is extinguished, although occasionally the fire goes out and needs to be relighted.

This fire is an amazing source of reliable heat. But it seems that so much of the energy is wasted. The top of the stove serves as a storehouse of potential heat, so we use it whenever possible. Water is boiled here for dishes. At night, a pot boils in a simmering burble, providing added humidity to the dry winter air. On some days, a large, lidded pan serves as a miniature oven, with warm rocks on the lid to aid the convection. Maybe this design can be improved upon.

Margy buys a toaster oven at a second-hand store for four dollars. It comes with a 5-day warranty. Take it home, and if it doesn't work, just bring it back. But Margy voids the warranty by tearing out the electronic guts of the oven. She removes the side panels and all of the wiring, so the toaster can be placed on top of the wood stove without melting plastic and rubber components. I insist she leave the functionless plastic timer knob. I want to move this lever for special effect when I heat my cinnamon roll. It continues to work reliably, despite the brutality of the heat from the wood stove.

On its first test flight, Margy tries some cornbread. It's a toaster oven with a slow warmup, since the original design was to prevent heat from leaving the oven. Now we want the heat to get in, and it does, though slowly. Once the heating process begins, it works like a charm, and we harness some of the stove's otherwise wasted energy. Too bad we can't figure out how to use the stove to generate electricity.

* * * * *

On Christmas Day, we invite John to an early dinner at our condo. With obvious hesitation, he accepts. I don't push him, since I know John's family attempts to tone down holidays as much as possible. I too have learned that is a wise approach for maintaining my peace of mind. I assume John's hesitancy today is related to the nature of the holidays.

This meal is a rare event for us, home cooking with all of the trimmings. The turkey Margy selects is way too large for the three of us (four with Bro at the table begging for scraps). The meal is served buffet-style, and John and I take huge helpings from the platters of turkey and bowls of dressing, peas, mashed potatoes, and gravy. We both go back for seconds.

As Margy is clearing the dishes, John and I go to the living room. Warm flames dance in the gas fireplace. We stand with our backs to the fire, looking out at the harbour through the patio door.

"Hey, Wayne, there's your boat," says John. His gaze is focused towards the end of the marina. I know "your boat" means what it always means.

"Which one?" I ask.

"Just to the right of the last dock gate. It's the first boat on the first ramp to the right. That's the boat you need, and it's for sale."

"What color?" I ask, straining to see the ramp he's talking about.

"Blue cover on the command bridge. The rest of it is white, except the lower hull paint is dark blue, almost black. Looks like a Commander, probably a 30-footer."

I can see some boats that look like small dots along the ramp. I'm pretty sure I know which boat John is referring to, but I certainly can't identify the colors or any design characteristics from here. My eyes can't compare with John's eagle vision, and it frustrates him when I can't see the details he notices.

"The problem is you already found a too-perfect boat for us," I remind him, referring to the Bayliner. "How could we ever sell her, no matter how good another boat is?"

John is forever looking for new (old) boats. He is insistent we need a bigger boat for the inlets to the north.

"We should go take a look at it," says John. "It's big enough to be a twin diesel, and maybe the price is right."

"How do you know it's for sale?"

"There's a 'For Sale' sign in the window," says John. "No price though."

No way! I can barely see the boat, and John can see a "For Sale" sign in the window? I grab the binoculars from the shelf and focus them on the dock. I work my way to the right, to the blue and white boat. It does look like a Commander. Focusing precisely with both eyepieces, I can barely see a rectangular sign in the window, but I certainly can't read "For Sale," even at seven-power magnification.

"Okay, do you want to walk down there, right now?" I give in.

"Would like to," replies John. "But Bro and I should go home now. Sorry to eat and run. The meal was great, but I promised to be home for Mom's Christmas dinner, and it will be served soon."

I bet he goes for seconds.

◊ ◊ ◊ ◊ ◊ ◊

Chapter 12

Winch It

John wants to see if we can get to the top of Blue Ridge in the snow. The recent January rains in Powell River have left the nearby mountains covered in white. Blue Ridge can be a challenge, even in the best conditions. Today I find it difficult to imagine we will make it all the way up this route on our quads. Maybe we can get close enough to finish off the climb with a hike to the top. The last portion of the trail is the steepest, so this may become a major effort.

The Granite Lake trail is the starting point. It becomes covered with snow a third of the way up to the lake. John and Bro lead Margy and me with no difficulties, except those caused by overhanging alders. With the weight of recent snow, branches hang across the trail, making the going slow. You can pull down on the branches, and they rebound, throwing off the snow in big chunks. This is a good way to get doused in the white stuff. Since John leads the way and prefers to stay dry (Bro heartily agrees), we stop every 50 meters or so to prune the branches. It will also make the route better for riders on future trips.

Nearing Granite Lake, the snow depth approaches a foot, but our quads are still doing well. Margy becomes temporarily stuck in a trench with her two-wheel drive Honda. I am able to assist, by hopping off my quad and giving her a push out of the rough spot. Her light bike may not have a lot of power and traction, but it's hard to find a spot where a strong push won't get her moving again.

John stops and works at the branches with his pruning shears in pause-and-go fashion. I hop off my quad and offer to clip for a while. John can still lead with his quad, as I walk ahead of him with the clippers. After I've made some progress, I return for my bike and pull ahead a little farther. John is pleased to be able to relax for a while, as I share the grunt-work.

I barely get started with the shears when I hear a quad behind us. John walks back to discuss things with the rider of a metallic maroon Grizzly, while I continue my work. John returns to explain that the rider wants to go around our quads, and push on ahead of us towards Blue Ridge.

We drive forward to find a spot on the trail to pull over far enough to allow the Grizz to pass. This quad has a windshield to protect the rider from the snowy, low-hanging branches. He'll knock the snow off for us, as the boughs rebound off his windshield, and his tracks will make the route easier for us to follow. In heavy snow, the first bike through has the most work to do.

After the maroon quad passes, John leads us past Granite Lake. Margy rides behind him, and I bring up the rear. Margy's quad has less ground clearance than bigger bikes, and pretty soon she is scraping the belly of her quad on the snow in the center of the path. Her tires spin helplessly in a few spots, but I am able to hop off my bike and push her through.

The snow deepens, and soon even my pushing won't get the Honda moving. Margy's rear tires spin aimlessly, the underbelly wedged on the trail's center hump of packed snow. The only solution is for Margy to get off her quad, and then we lift the bike's rear end out of the snow tracks. In fresh snow at the side of the trail, she finds new traction. This solves the problem, until the next time, and the next. The procedure gets old quickly, as we begin to sweat in our heavy jackets.

Fortunately, we don't have to put up with this much longer. We are brought to a stop by the maroon Grizz, stuck in a cross-trench. He's mired more in mud than snow. Even his four-wheel drive and differential lockers won't get him free of the deep rut.

John hooks up the cable from his winch to free the quad. With special interest, I watch him connect the cable to the maroon bike's rear end. In two years of riding in the bush, I've never seen a winch used in an actual rescue operation. When I purchased my quad, John insisted a winch be included with the accessories. I've only tested it once, by attaching the cable to a tree and pulling myself along a short stretch of flat trail.

After hooking up the cable, John hops back aboard his quad. He stands on his running boards, and hits the retraction switch with his left hand, using his right hand to lock his front brake. The guy in the stuck quad uses his reverse power, in concert with the winch's retraction, to slowly back out of the trench. What would this rider have done if we hadn't come along?

Once free, the maroon quad is able to turn around. We begin the process of reversing course too. No one is going to make it any farther on this trail today.

Getting turned around is a slow process in the snow. The quads want to remain in their snow tracks, and the trail is barely wide enough for course reversal. I back up a ways to find a wider spot, and I manage to get turned around. Then I walk back to assist Margy. In her case, it's a simple matter of lifting her quad out of the snow tracks and rocking the bike around in the middle of the trail, until it is headed back downhill.

I lead now, and John instructs me to turn at the Granite Lake turnoff, about a half-kilometer back down the trail. I pull off onto the spur and wait for the rest of the riders. I wave Margy and John down to the lake, while I sit at the intersection. I want to make sure the maroon Grizz gets out of the heavy snow without further problems. In a few more seconds, the quad passes me; he waves and continues down the main trail.

At the lake, we eat our lunch and discuss our revised plans. We still have four hours of daylight, and John knows a nearby trail that will be challenging, yet below our snow limit.

Granite Lake is slushy near the shoreline, obviously not frozen solid. I visited here the previous winter, when there was less snow on the ground, but solid ice on the lake. The recent weather has been wet and mild, leaving lots of snow at higher elevations, but not much ice.

"Wasn't that kind of dangerous for that rider to try this route solo today?" I ask. I know John has a conservative approach to riding safety, so I'm sure he will be critical of the rider's decision to press on alone in these conditions. If we had turned back before finding the maroon Grizz, he might have been stranded on a snowy mountain, a long way from help.

"It's a bit risky," John replies. "But he seems like an experienced rider."

"I doubt a cell phone would work here," I point out. "And he wouldn't have gotten out of that trench without your winch."

I'm always more comfortable in this area when carrying my satellite phone, although I haven't needed to use it in an emergency, yet. Few others in this region carry such a phone.

"If you know what you're doing, you can work at it to free your quad," says John. "You can dig yourself out of almost any spot, but it takes a lot of work. He might have been able to use his own winch to pull himself out."

John knows more about this than I do. It still seems perilous to travel by yourself in snow like this. In fact, solo riding in remote areas (which John does regularly) seems risky, under any conditions. Then again, I ponder how much I enjoy boating and hiking by myself, a long way from civilization. There's just something special about being alone with nature in the wilderness.

Before we leave the lake, I pose a challenge to John. I can never determine directions accurately after weaving around on trails, unless there is an obvious angle to the sun for a point of reference. Today it is completely overcast, even a bit foggy here, with no evidence of the direction to the sun. We sit in the tops of clouds.

"Try this," I say. "Turn and face north."

John looks at me kind of funny and then obliges. He faces out across the lake at an oblique angle. He loves a challenge.

I would have guessed north is in a completely different direction. There is no doubt John is right, and I am wrong. He has an uncanny sense of location wherever he goes.

I step up next to John and show him my recent Christmas present. It's a sporty-looking electronic compass, compact and digital.

"Hold out your hands – straight out in front of you" I instruct, and John does just that.

I put the compass in John's outstretched hands, as he stands facing across the lake. I flick the compass switch to the "On" position. The compass digital display illuminates. It reads "355."

"Not bad," I smirk. "You're inaccurate by only 5 degrees."

John smiles and brags: "Maybe the compass is off a bit."

"Probably." We both laugh.

After our lunch stop, John leads us back down the Granite Lake trail. Near the bottom, we make a turnoff to the left. At the next split in the trail, he stops. Margy and I pull up beside him in the wide junction.

"I've only been on this trail once before," he announces. For John, that makes this route unique.

"Is it a tough trail?" I ask.

"Not that I remember." John remembers everything. Maybe this means he doesn't want to scare me.

We continue past the split in the trail, and John stays to the right. Then we approach another "Y," and John stops to survey the intersection. He looks up the trail to the left. It leads up a steep hill. The path to the right heads downhill, at least at first. Seldom does John ponder which way to turn. I assume it is because he knows both trails, but is trying to decide which route will be better today.

His decision made, we peel off to the right. At first, it's a nice winding trail. Then it curves through a logging slash, narrows, and comes to an end. Ahead is a wide swampy area that looks impassible on a quad.

"Wrong road," says John. "I made the wrong turn, so we need to go back." This is a momentous occasion. Never before have I seen John, even momentarily, not know exactly where he is. We're not lost, but we're as close as I'd ever expect to be with John.

We turn around and return to the intersection, taking the uphill route this time. It winds upward into snow-covered terrain that approaches the depth we experienced above Granite Lake. At one spot, we pause while Brody gets a break from his aft-mounted quad box. As Bro runs around sniffing at the bushes in the snow, I express my concern:

"The snow's getting pretty deep. It's almost at the limit of Margy's bike."

"It won't get any deeper," replies John matter-of-factly. "We're almost to the top of the ridge. Then we start down again." Spoken like a person who knows exactly where he is.

"I hope you're right," Margy chimes in.

"Count on it," says John. "I was here several years ago, and I remember the trees."

That's John – he remembers things like trees. He'll never get lost when he remembers trees.

Sure enough, we continue upward for only a short stretch. John stops adjacent to an open area to our right. When Margy and I pull up near him, he explains this is the location of an old railroad bed, used for logging. I can pick out a straight stretch, now that he mentions it. Without John's guidance, it would have been hidden from view by my lack of attention to details.

Another 100 meters up the trail, we stop at an overlook to enjoy the majestic view.

"What's that body of water?" asks John. He's testing me.

It's big, but it doesn't look familiar. It could be Lois Lake, but I think we're too far from Lois to see it from here.

"Haslam Lake," I say, trying to sound confident.

"Not even close – we're looking south, not west. That's Texada on the other side of the water."

We're looking across Malaspina Strait at Texada Island. It's not even a lake – it's an ocean. Where's my mental compass?

We start downhill, and the trail gets more challenging. The snow nearly disappears, but the path gets narrow and steep. There are scrapes on the trees where quads have cut the sharp turns a little too close. The scars are old and nearly healed, indicating few have passed along this trail in recent weeks.

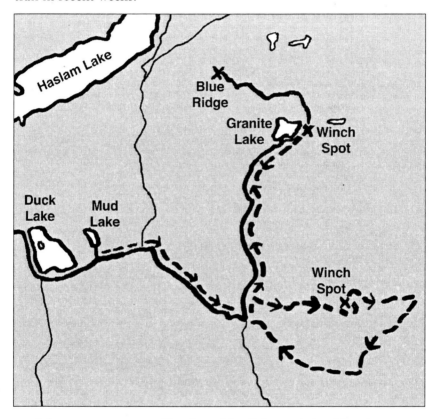

John stops to remove Bro from his aft box, setting him down next to the quad. When Bro is asked to walk rather than ride, it's a clear indication the trail is getting rough, almost to the limit of a quad. John knows when Bro is about to be thrown out of his box by steep, rough terrain. He anticipates those conditions now.

As Bro explores ahead of John, I watch them approach the headwaters of Suicide Creek. The upslope on the other side of the stream is steep. Not only is the creek's trench deep, the other side is dark brown, almost black. That's an indicator of muddy conditions. Mud and uphill grade are not a good combination.

Margy stops in front of me to watch John pass through the creek and up the other side. In tough spots, it's always wise to study John's specific route, and then follow it.

John chooses the path of least resistance. But, in this case, it is not good enough. He is in four-wheel drive now. But a deep and muddy rut on the left side of the incline brings John to a halt. He backs up a few feet and attacks it again. And again. I bet his lockers are engaged now. He isn't going any farther. And when John can't go any farther, you know it's a really tough spot.

I shut off my engine and walk forward past Margy to discuss the situation with John. He is already reeling out his winch cable and walking uphill to find a tree in-line with the trail. His left wheels are stuck in a deep rut, his front tire resting against a boulder imbedded in the top of the rut.

"Need to winch myself out," says John, much like you or I would say: "Need to walk a little faster," when we are late for an appointment. He hops back on his quad, and takes up the slack in the winch cable. He pushes on his throttle just enough to keep up with the retracting cable. His bike rises gradually and smoothly over the rock, tipping the quad high and to the right. John leans far left to compensate, and the quad moves slowly but safely past this nasty spot in the trail.

Once over the rock, he continues to winch himself upward for a few more feet. The remaining upslope is steep but much smoother, drier too. John stops the winch and drives forward to relieve the tension in the cable. He hops off his quad and disconnects the cable from the tree. Then he retracts the winch cable the rest of the way.

John drives the remaining thirty feet to the top of the hill and maneuvers his quad around, facing downhill. He's ready for the next customer. The next customer is Margy, and she doesn't have a winch.

John and I walk back down to Margy's quad to discuss the plan to get her through the tough spot. She sits, engine off, on the far side of the creek. Margy is a bit apprehensive about being winched up a hill. But she puts on a brave face, and promptly starts her engine. She moves into position, by crossing the creek and climbing a few feet on the other side. She stops short of the offending rut and boulder. John returns to his bike, and brings his winch cable down to her quad. He connects the cable to the front of the Honda's frame.

"It's important to give 'er just enough power to keep up with the cable, as I retract it," instructs John. "If you see any slack developing, ease off the power right away. Keep the cable nice and tight, but help the winch by using just enough throttle to keep up with it."

Margy acknowledges, without any questions. She's showing her plucky side. If John says this is the way it has to be done, there is no doubt. At times like this, it's nice to have complete faith in a leader.

All goes well, much smoother than I would have guessed. While John retracts the winch and Margy contributes a little power, I push on the quad's rear for good measure. She glides gently up and over the granite obstacle, and then slowly climbs up the remainder of the hill.

Now it's my turn.

But first I want to try the slope without using a winch. Two quads have smoothed things a bit, so there's a chance I can make it through in four-wheel drive, even though John couldn't.

On my first attempt, I am a bit hesitant with the throttle, and I don't even come close to making it through the rut. I back up and try again. This time, with more aggressive throttle, I make it halfway up the rocky rut, but then come to an abrupt halt, with my tires spinning helplessly.

One more try. This time I back up a bit farther, and take an even bigger run at the rough spot. I hit the boulder at the end of the rut with a jolt. My quad stops precariously tilted to the right, at the limit of my comfort zone. As I try to back up, my heart pounds. My wheels spin, and I am stuck. It's time for the winch.

Rather than use John's cable to pull me up the hill, I want to use my own winch. This will be my first real attempt to extract myself from an otherwise go-no-farther situation. John helps me release the winch's clutch and pull the cable up the hill to the awaiting tree. Then I climb back on my quad and retract the cable to a taut position. I apply a bit of throttle with my right thumb, while retracting the winch cable with my left thumb. Slowly, and amazingly smoothly, I ride up and over the boulder. For practice, I continue winching myself up the remainder of the hill, until I am only a few feet from the anchor tree.

Ahead, the path looks a lot better, although it remains narrow. At a split in the trail, John turns left. Before proceeding, we stop to inspect a rusty object at the side of the intersection. To me it looks like an old metal stove, rounded at the top.

"It's an old spark arrestor from a locomotive," says John. How does he know these things?

John's decision regarding a left turn leads us to a dead end. We end up in a turnaround spot where the trees close in around us. Ahead and to our right, an old trail continues, but today it is completely flooded and running like a river.

"Wrong turn," says John. You don't hear him say that very often. Today I have heard it twice. Quick, write that down.

"I don't remember these trees," says John. "Must be the other way." We reverse course, pass the spark arrestor, and continue down the trail on the other spur. Now we are in the heart of an old logging area. In an open area beneath the forest canopy, giant stumps surround us. Scattered patches of snow mingle with mossy logs. It's park-like.

The path widens more, and there are red, triangular trail markers embedded in the trees. We are, for a few hundred meters, on a segment of the Sunshine Coast Trail, which junctions with Conchie Road. From here, it will be an easy ride back to our starting point at the entrance to Granite Lake Road.

As we pop out of the forest onto Conchie Road, we are clearly back in John's well-traveled territory. In fact, hand-made wooden signs mark the intersection. I turn around and read the sign designating the entrance to the trail we have just exited: "Suicide Pass." It seems an appropriate name for an area impossible to ride today without a winch.

Chapter 13

970-Millibar Low

At all times aboard a floating cabin, it is best to expect strong winds. It takes awhile to learn the lessons of wind ignorance.

Twenty-gallon plastic buckets prove themselves as excellent storage containers for a variety of objects, including kindling wood. One of my regular chores is to collect driftwood that arrives on the ebb and flow of the gentle waters in the Hole. Some of this wood is cut up, with my chainsaw, for firewood. Most is small enough to toss into one of the large plastic buckets, which are strategically placed around the float.

One evening, I finish my propane-heated shower out on the deck, using one of the blue 20-gallon buckets. Rather than empty the large bucket and drag it back inside, I leave it on the deck, half-filled with water to prevent the wind from sweeping it away. That's about 10 gallons of water, over 60 pounds.

During the night, the heavy bucket of water disappears. Similarly, smaller 9-liter buckets also depart the deck regularly during our first weeks of cabin ownership. It takes awhile to learn the lesson – if it isn't bolted down, the wind will remove it from the deck.

A full year after losing the big blue bucket, John and his friend, Doug, are installing additional flotation barrels under one corner of Cabin Number 3's float structure. The modification is necessary because heavy firewood is stored in that corner of the cabin. Doug dives with his scuba gear, finding a variety of old items. Wedged under the float is the large blue shower bucket.

* * * * *

One morning, after a moderate windstorm, I awake to find a huge green caterpillar in the natural swimming pool behind the cabin. No, it is not the USO (Underwater Swimming Object) I've long suspected lives in this lake. Yes, it is huge (8 feet long); and yes, it is a caterpillar (the plastic water-toy variety). It has floated inside the confines of tethered logs that mark the boundary of my swimming area. I conclude it was blown into the pool from the cabin around the corner. Beyond the old trailer shed on floats (lovingly referred to as "Trashy Trailer"), twin girls live with their parents in the nearby cabin. The twins will be shattered to learn of the loss of their caterpillar.

Today, I depart for town soon after dawn. So as I leave the Hole, I drop the toy caterpillar at their cabin, tying it to their breakwater. Here is proof – if it isn't tied down, it's gonna leave. That even includes giant caterpillars.

* * * * *

The number of objects that have flown out of the rear of the Campion is mind-boggling. You'd think I would learn to be more careful after losing a few valuable items. But the amount of suction created at even moderate speeds surprises me. When I leave the center windshield open, air swirls through the boat and out the stern. The list of lost items ranges from bags of garbage (very disconcerting, since I feel protective of the lake's eco-system) to a valuable pair of blue jeans

Margy has secured under a 2-gallon jug of water. In such instances, I watch the objects depart, as if in slow motion. Even with an immediate course reversal, locating them on the water's surface before sinking is usually impossible. Sometimes John finds these times during his regular beachcombing runs.

John is a perpetual beachcomber. In fact, that is his specialty. He misses nothing as he cruises up and down the lake. Specific trips are reserved just for checking the shoreline for new treasures. After a major storm, you'll find him out on the lake, surveying for new arrivals. He'll then tow a floating set of stairs (maybe broken off from a float cabin), all the way across the lake at a snail's pace. His favorite place to stash such stuff is Cabin Number 1.

One day, John proudly announces the discovery of a boat paddle in the inner bay of the Hole. I'm surprised he isn't reporting the discovery of Margy's blue jeans. John is worried I'll claim the paddle, since it looks similar to one from the Campion, and he's relieved that it is not.

John tells me about a recent prize from the lower lake— an olive-drab life vest, similar to those I use in the Campion. He discovered it floating in Three-Mile Bay. Since I have not reported the loss of a life vest, he feels assured the badly deteriorated vest is not mine. I don't have the heart to tell him I've been missing a life vest for several months. I didn't think such an object would exit my boat in the draft of cruise flight. If something isn't strapped down in the Campion, it goes airborne. In this instance, for the sake of friendship, a water-soaked white lie seems appropriate.

* * * * *

Fall and winter storms on the BC coast rival the biggest storms anywhere. In fact, the word "hurricane" could describe some of these storms, were it not for one minor technicality. Like hurricanes, these storms are intense low pressure centers (cyclones) with adequate velocity to be classed as a hurricane – winds at least 120 kilometers per hour. But the giants that arise in the Gulf of Alaska and move inland along the BC coast are extratropical cyclones, originating outside the warm waters of the tropics. By definition, intensity alone cannot qualify these giants as tropical cyclones (hurricanes). Otherwise, they are huge storms.

BC winter storms are, in fact, much larger than hurricanes, typically spanning a thousand kilometers or more. Also unlike hurricanes, they incorporate violent frontal systems, usually cold fronts. These storm zones ravage the BC coast with winds, waves, and rain. They often back up, one behind the other, far out into the Pacific. The result is week-after-week of winter torment for the coast.

During two consecutive boat trips to our float cabin in January, Margy and I manage to barely beat the incoming storms. If you act fast enough, you can get lucky with a sprint up the lake. Usually, these monster storms back into Powell River from the southeast. The circulation around the low is anticlockwise (counterclockwise for you Americans), so the storm is first felt moving in on southeast winds, up the Strait of Georgia. Storms coming down the coast arrive by the back door in the pinwheel swirl of the cyclone.

To get lucky three times in a row is pushing it. Margy and I rush through the checkout line at the grocery store, and load our bags of food in the truck. The already-gusting southeast winds and swirling drops of rain pound the parking lot. If we hurry, we may be able to outrun the storm as it moves into town and then migrates quickly up the lake.

Our route out of town crisscrosses through Cranberry and the edge of the Powell River townsite, then north to the Shinglemill. It's an even race with the developing storm. We load the boat in the gusty wind and rain that has followed us from town. But once on the lake, it is a straight shot north to Hole in the Wall. We may outrun the frontal system again. Our 30-klick speed in the Campion barely outpaces the storm. We're winning again!

By the time we reach John's Cabin Number 1, the rain has almost stopped, and even the waves are cooperating. The North Sea, typically the roughest part of the trip, is amazingly smooth. One-foot wind waves barely slow our progress. By First Narrows, it is almost calm.

As we pull into the cabin's breakwater, I notice a 10-foot-long log floating next to the stump known as Elephant Butt. This log is begging to come aboard as firewood. It will be hard to pass up, since its narrow girth is perfect for cutting. The log won't even need splitting to meet the dimensions of the fireplace. But first, before the rain hits, it's important to get everything off-loaded from the boat.

As always, we carry a lot of stuff during this trip to the cabin. Besides eight small bags of groceries, we haul our backpacks, laptop computers, two 8-liter containers of water, a large bag of clean laundry, and two containers of gasoline. We off-load quickly, barely beating the storm. By the time I make my walk-around inspection of the float decks, turn on the electrical inverter, and extend the gangplank to shore, it is already starting to rain. Maybe the tempting log will hang around near the cabin until I can snag it during the first pause in the storm.

Once inside the cabin, my first check involves the propane refrigerator. The propane bottle wasn't expected to outlast our three-day stay in town, but it is a shame to waste even a little stored energy. Thus, I have left the nearly empty bottle connected. The refrigerator holds its temperature well this time of the year, even if the propane runs out during our absence. (I'm still dumb-founded by the efficiency of propane refrigerators, making cold by burning gas.)

No surprise – I open the refrigerator door and find the blue reflection tab no longer glowing, indicating the flame is extinguished. A quick check of the freezer verifies the ice cubes are just beginning to melt, and the meat is still nicely frozen. It will be a simple matter of switching propane tanks and relighting the fridge.

Well, maybe not that simple. I've finally got the reverse-thread aspect of propane fittings down to a science. But swapping two large bottles, in the confined quarters of their outside storage shed, is always a challenge. All goes well at first, as the wooden side-panel comes off easily. The fitting on the old bottle comes loose without difficulty. I move the empty bottle next to the Campion for loading. By now, the rain has changed from spotty showers to a steady downpour, and I'm getting soaked.

I lift the spare bottle onto its wooden platform, which aligns it with the attachment tube and fitting. When they line up properly, it's an almost-automatic finger-spin onto the bottle. But the bottle isn't aligned properly, and I can't seem to get it into the correct position. I fiddle with the fitting in the cramped space within the shed, trying to get the threads started by-hand. It's important not to force it, to avoid stripping the soft brass threads. I twist and twist, and the fitting just won't line up properly. I can feel the threads trying to engage, but a hundred soft twists accomplish nothing.

I move the bottle, reposition the fitting, and carefully push it against the edge of the threads. Still, the fitting will not engage. A trip into the cabin for some Vaseline lubricant is a wise decision. It reminds me how careful I need to be with these threads to avoid stripping them. But the refrigerator needs propane!

The trip into the cabin is a huge relief from the cold and wet, but I shouldn't stay long. The rain is getting heavier, so the job is not going to get any easier with time.

Another half-hour goes by before the threads finally engage and smoothly snug together. It's nothing I do differently that solves the problem. It's simply a matter of patient persistence until the threads are ready to join of their own accord.

By now I am thoroughly soaked and chilled. Wisely, I take a few extra minutes to secure the old propane bottle in the Campion and fasten all of the boat's canvas snaps. I lost an empty propane bottle once in the wind, overboard from the cabin deck. John wasn't happy.

Margy has started the wood fire, so it is a warm, dry relief inside the cabin. I immediately go into a coughing fit, not my common reaction from coming in out of the cold and wet. But if there ever was a surefire way to catch pneumonia, this is it. I visualize the Coast Guard launching their inflatable boat from the Shinglemill during a major gale, to rescue me from the Hole. They haul me off the float on a stretcher, and then to the hospital in town. We speed away from Number 3 in the rubber boat, waves crashing. I have a vivid imagination.

Within a few hours, darkness falls and the rain lets up. I cough a lot, a condition undoubtedly enhanced by my imagination. A storm is moving in, we will be stranded at the float for at least a day, and I am coming down with pneumonia!

At first, the storm moves in slowly. Then, the wind rises from the east, pushing over and down the face of Goat Island. The blast of air charges across the narrow channel, towards the Hole. The surge in wind is accompanied by the low-frequency hum of the wind generator blades spinning up. A major winter storm is roaring in fast.

Pilots are weather junkies, and I'm no exception. Flight safety is partly dictated by the whims of the air, so I pay attention to the weather. Boaters are a similar breed. So it's not surprising I've developed a miniature weather station at the cabin. Tonight, the initial storm data on my digital displays is intriguing. The temperature is 3 degrees C, with the trend arrow upward. The barometer is low, and falling fast. Already, the pressure reading is 998 millibars, well below the standard of 1013.

On the cabin wall, an old-fashioned aneroid barometer backs up my digital pressure reading. I tap the instrument's glass, and the needle jumps downward. It's a straight-forward indication of falling pressure, as my tap releases the aneroid's spring-tension.

The wind is howling now, accompanied by the thrum of the wind generator's blades. I step out onto the deck, raising my hand-held anemometer up into the wind. It registers 17.6 miles per hour. I walk back along the side of the cabin to the wind generator and gaze upward at the rotating blades. The orange on-speed light glows bright on the bottom of the dull steel casing. We're making electricity!

Back inside, I study the voltmeter, as the batteries register a significant charge. The voltage is already holding at 12.4, and then a strong gust hits. I hear the generator's blades hum more loudly and watch the voltmeter jump upward to 12.6. Now 12.8, and then abruptly 13.4, as the wind howls outside. Suddenly, the volts drop back to 12.4 as the generator's blades go into their stalled position, and I hear them abruptly spin down. Technically, this should happen well before 13.4 volts, but the gusts are strong, and even the overvoltage regulator can't keep pace.

The marine radio station, broadcasting from Texada Island, is easily picked up from Hole in the Wall, although it typically takes a bit of antenna tilting to get a clear signal. Usually, the volume peaks and fades, unless I hold onto the radio, using my body as an additional antenna. Tonight, the signal is particularly fickle, but the reports I catch are exciting. Sentry Shoal, near Savary Island, is a nearby benchmark location. The winds there are already blowing from the southeast at 30, gusting to 42. Velocity is reported in knots, so that equates to gusts up to 78 kilometers per hour. The barometer at Sentry Shoal is 987.5 millibars, and falling. This storm is moving in fast.

Grief Point is another benchmark, although only wind speed is reported there – 35 knots, gusting to 45. The marine weather summary places a 970-millibar low 200 miles west of Cape Scott. That's a mighty intense extratropical cyclone. The low is forecasted to move across central Vancouver Island by early morning. Normally, storms this time of year move down the coast from the Gulf of Alaska. But this one is moving inland from a warmer region of the Pacific. The milder conditions should prevent snow at our elevation, but warm air can hold more moisture than cold air. So this is an intense cyclone, with closely-spaced isobars (indicating strong winds) and lots of rain.

At 9 PM, the wind increases. My clothesline-flag-estimate is 70 kilometers per hour, with considerably stronger gusts. I'm tempted to step out onto the deck for a more accurate anemometer reading, but the wind is strong and the deck is slippery. The gusts are so strong that they could actually sweep me from the deck. So I huddle inside, watch the weather gauges, and keep my radio tuned to the marine reports. I cough a bit to simulate pneumonia. Hypochondriac extraordinaire.

When winds are from the southeast, our cabin pushes on the stiff leg, a hefty log designed to keep us from pounding up against the cliff. This also establishes a steady force against the shore, and the cabin remains fairly stationary. But the conditions tonight are gusty, with rapid changes in both velocity and direction. When the wind shifts to any direction other than southeast, the cabin swings away from the cliff. Then we float outward to the maximum length of the shoreline cables.

Fortunately, John has installed dual cables at each connection. When the cables extend to their limit, they mutually absorb the shock. There are still minor jolts as the cabin jerks to a stop, but it is less severe with doubled cables. And, if a cable should break, it's a lot safer.

As the wind swirls within the Hole, the jolts increase. Wind direction can change in an instant, diverted by the cliff to strike the cabin at an entirely different angle. We go for a ride, this way and that. Every few cycles, we jar to a sudden stop. It's not enough to throw things off the shelves, but it's best to be sitting down when the cables reach their limit.

John has built a sturdy cabin, a marvel of engineering. How the metal roof stays on in winds like this is beyond my understanding. To say nothing of why flying debris has never broken a window or glass door.

In the Hole tonight, I hear firewood logs rolling around on the deck. Branches must be falling off the 100-foot cliff and tumbling in unexpected directions. But nothing impacts our secure shelter.

When I go to bed, the barometric pressure is still dropping, now 985 millibars. It is a fitful sleep. The wind howls, and the rain lashes the cabin roof and walls. The wind generator's blades change pitch, as they speed up and then stall suddenly in the gusty conditions. It is both nerve-wracking and comforting. There's something about being warm and dry in a floating cabin during a raging storm.

Occasionally, the cables yank taut, and a jolt jars me awake. By 2 AM, the jolts are more closely spaced, indicating the wind has switched direction. I climb down from the loft, and carefully step out onto the deck. The wind is howling down the cliff next to the cabin, pushing downward and outward to the south. I doubt the wind is actually from the north, but the swirl against the cliff redirects the airflow, pushing the cabin and its breakwater logs out into the channel.

The rain has stopped. As I stand on the deck, in what seems like only a few minutes, the clouds break up. The wind nearly disappears. Overhead, stars appear.

The clearing has been rapid. Could this be the very center of the low, not unlike the eye of a hurricane? Extratropical cyclones also have an eye, although it's not normally clearly defined. A check of my weather gauges raises questions. The pressure has dropped to 979 millibars and is holding steady. That's a bit higher than the forecast center of the cyclone, although the low could be filling now. The storm has made landfall, and air is rushing in from all sides. The temperature has increased considerably, up from 3 degrees to 8 degrees C, in the past few hours. Such warming at night is not typical, so I conclude we are in the northeast quadrant of the storm, where a warm front would lie.

Back inside the cabin, the radio's marine forecast is old, from 9:30 PM. A new forecast will not be issued until 4 AM. But the individual station reports are up to date. Sentry Shoal registers 45-knot winds from the southeast with gusts, and barometric pressure 982 and steady. Grief Point reports winds from the southeast at 40 knots, gusting to 50. These gusts equate to 93 klicks, and that's about as close to hurricane force as I care to witness.

In the Hole, wind is quickly picking up again. I step back out onto the deck, but I huddle near the patio door, an area protected from the full force of the wind. In front of me, where it was nearly calm only minutes ago, two-foot waves are crashing against the breakwater. The waves easily breach the barrier, and then crash again against the cabin's brow logs. Water splashes everywhere.

I shine my flashlight towards the transition float. The gangplank to shore has been thrown off the float. It bobs in the water, waves slapping back and forth over it. An attached rope will keep it within reach for morning. I'm not going out into this storm to retrieve a gangplank.

I shine my light between the cabin and the cliff. The stiff leg is floating free now, and the cabin heaves to and fro on the cables. In the middle of the natural swimming pool bobs a big log. It's the log I first saw floating near Elephant Butt the previous afternoon. The storm has chased it into more-protected waters.

I light the fireplace and watch the orange flames dance in the disturbed air within the stove. The updraft of the chimney pulls the flames up towards the unstable air passing over the cabin. The result is a particularly attractive fire. I scratch out a rough cough that hurts my throat, reminding me that my pneumonia is real. Or is it?

I hear the rain approaching again. Like a train in the distance, it roars across the gap from Goat Island. Heavy drops hit the metal roof, announcing its arrival. In a matter of minutes, the weather has gone from calm and nearly clear to threatening wind and heavy rain. The eye has passed.

I sit on the couch, watching the fire, and listening to the marine weather radio. I check the trends in temperature and pressure on my mini weather station. The barometer has stabilized at 976 millibars and remains there for the next few hours. The temperature begins to drop quickly, finally leveling off at 2 degrees C, indicating passage of the cold front. We now are on the west side of the low, the storm roaring on towards Vancouver.

I stay awake until 4 AM, catch the updated marine forecast, and observe the winds die down again to a light breeze. As I catnap on the couch, the rain continues throughout the early morning hours.

I am beginning to feel better now. The improving weather is probably influencing my perceived health. And my ability to return to town, now that the storm has passed, relaxes me. I am no longer deathly ill. The mind behaves in strange ways.

Near sunrise, I check the rain gauge – 1.6 inches in the past 12 hours. Water is pouring off Goat, tumbling in four distinct waterfalls observable from the front deck. Another small waterfall flows down the nearby cliff steps, pouring off the stairs in a cascade. John built these steps in a natural gully in the cliff. This morning, the channel has reverted to its original function.

The 8 AM marine forecast includes a mid-channel report from the Queen of Burnaby, the first Comox to Powell River ferry crossing of the day: "Wind south at 40 knots, gusting. Pressure 983 and rising, with 7-foot seas. Rough." I bet it is "rough" in the Strait of Georgia this morning, and I'm glad I'm in my cabin. The storm has passed, but it will take the entire morning for the winds and waves to die down. Gradually, the coastal airflow will recover. In its wake, the low pressure system leaves a clear reminder of the power of the weather.

As the morning progresses, Hole in the Wall returns to its normal tranquility. My pneumonia is now a routine cold. The Coast Guard will not need to rescue me after all.

Chapter 14

Goat 2

Mid-October's weather is consistent rain, and I'm waiting for a break. The evening brings showers to Powell River, with visible breaks in the clouds to the west over Vancouver Island. The local forecast calls for two days of sunny breaks starting tomorrow. I'm skeptical. The long-range forecast on TV portrays little cloud symbols, with rain protruding below for the next ten days.

The following morning dawns with more sunny breaks to the west. And the rain has stopped. I adjust the rabbit ears on our condo's miniature TV. Some days you can receive as many as three channels, but only Channel 13 is viewable today. The morning weather report begins with the satellite time-lapse view of coastal BC and Vancouver Island. The edge of the next frontal system is poised just offshore, but the forecaster insists Vancouver will eke out some sunny breaks today. The Sunshine Coast (Rain Coast) should be similarly spared. I'm still skeptical, but it's enough to prepare for a ride and hike.

John is intent on Goat 2, where he has been trying to push through a deactivated logging road. For the past several weeks, he's been working this trail during every acceptable weather break. On his last attempt, he couldn't convince anyone to join him (except Bro, of course), so he carefully went as far as he could go on his own. Finally, he reached a creek roaring in full flood. The violent flow ripped across the old road and dropped off the cliff on the other side. The water ran swift, and strong enough to take a quad with it.

John spent an hour throwing rocks into the stream, trying to reduce the depth of the water at the crossing spot. Finally he felt comfortable with the situation, and drove carefully across the creek ("Hang on, Bro!"). Then he pressed on to the turnout at the end of the old road.

From there, he hiked into the bush a bit farther to evaluate plans for future visits to this site.

Once John begins working a trail, he works it, and works it some more, until a new trail finally supersedes the project. Today it will be real work. The turnout past the creek is to become the start of another rejuvenated logging road, farther up the valley of Goat 2. I look forward to seeing Goat 2, but the grunt work sounds like drudgery. Also, it is a weekday, and that means logging trucks. On the way to Goat 2, we'll be riding on an active logging road, at least for a short stretch. John uses a VHF radio to communicate with the logging trucks, but travel on these roads during the week is still not recommended. Since John's radio earphone isn't working, we'll need to periodically stop, turn off our engines, and listen for traffic. Rick and John disassembled the radio last night, trying to find the source of the earphone's connection problem, with no success. What happens if a logging truck rams on through while we are riding rather than listening?

This morning, I awake from a nightmare in which a logging truck with a full load smashes into a blue quad (must be John's). Both vehicles sit in a mangled heap (primarily the quad, of course) in the middle of the road. John and the truck driver are in a violent argument, shaking their fists at each other. Bro is barking his head off at the driver. I wonder how much a logging truck costs?

Because the weather is so unsettled, we don't set a specific meeting time this morning, but I shoot for our standard 9:15 rendezvous at John's house. Margy and I hook up to the quad trailer at the airport, stop for breakfast, and then leisurely head for John's. We roll into the driveway at 9:17. John's truck is gone.

Rick's taxicab sits in the driveway, front wheels propped up on jacks. Both front tires are spinning, stopping, and spinning again.

"Your tires are spinning," I announce. Rick is half in and half out of the driver's seat, looking around the door jamb at the left front wheel.

"Sure are," replies Rick. "Front wheel drive, you know. Just checking the brakes." He pushes the gas pedal again, and then taps the brake. The wheels stop smoothly.

"What's wrong?" I ask.

"I think one of my rotors is grabbing, but I can't tell which one."

Rick is a brake nut. He's always worried about his brakes. If he worked in a muffler shop, he's the guy who would change all of your brakes, even though you came in for a new tail pipe.

"Where's John?" I ask.

"Gone looking for you at the airport," says Rick.

Oh, great – that means John is in a hurry. He has probably organized a trail-building crew, and he doesn't want to keep them waiting. Now we have the added pressure of keeping up with others on this trip. I've already decided I don't want to drive the short stretch on the active logging road, and I've been thinking about how to break the news to John.

Besides, I'm guessing that John is already worried about leaving Margy behind on the Goat 2 trail, if she can't make it through on her two-wheel drive quad. The limitation of her bike, coupled with her aversion to heights, could be a drag on our progress. With other bikers along, it will be stressful for all of us. Margy and I have repeatedly argued with John that Margy is content being left behind on the trail, exploring on her own and awaiting our return. John doesn't accept it: "Just ain't right," he says.

We don't have to wait long for John to return. He swings around the corner and rolls down the window of his truck, while still braking the F150 to a stop.

"Let's go!" he yells.

We follow John to the gas station and fill up the quads. Then I hop into John's truck for the ride to the off-load spot. Margy follows in her truck, pulling our quad trailer. There is something I want to discuss with John. It's okay if Bro overhears us.

I muster up the courage to admit I don't want to go to Goat 2 today. Margy and I can ride on other roads that are open to ATVs on a weekday, while John and his friends continue to Goat 2. But before I can say a thing, John announces that Bob is meeting us at Mud Lake. That changes everything.

Bob drives the biggest crew boat on Powell Lake, and he knows many of the area's loggers. He also knows logging road procedures. Bob is the gentlest guy you'll ever meet. Normally-calm John, on the other hand, can be a bit of a hothead in certain situations. One of those specific situations regards logging road access.

I've been replaying an incident in my mind this morning. It involves the Clover Lake logging dock, where John and I off-loaded our 100 cc motorcycles from John's boat for a ride on Goat Island (*Up the Lake*, Chapter 8). A logging boss, who doesn't want us there, meets us at the dock. John doesn't want the loggers there either, and he diplomatically explains that to the logging boss: "Whose forests are these?" he asks pointedly.

Of course, the answer is that the forests belong to all of us, but the logging boss doesn't want to hear it. After all, his company has the logging rights to this land. To make matters worse, these particular loggers work for an American company, which doesn't go over well with John. It almost becomes a bloody episode, which I am glad to escape.

At the dock, we off-load our motorcycles from the boat and ride up the hill. We pass the logging boss, standing beside the standard version of a trashy trailer. The glare from his piercing eyes is something to remember. I recall hoping we would find our boat still floating when we returned.

But Bob's presence neutralizes my fears. He's an ex-logger and all around easy-going guy. He'll know how to handle any encounter we have with a logging truck.

At the Mud Lake turnoff, Bob is already there, off-loaded and ready to go. John pulls into his normal parking spot among the trees, and Margy stops on the left shoulder of the road, not quite wide enough for an off-load spot. Bob approaches our truck to offer assistance, while Margy rolls down her window.

"Why don't you just back up a little, right down the road, and pull off on the opposite side," he says, pointing to a wide turnout on the other side of the road.

I too offer some help: "You'll need to turn your wheel to the right as you back up, to get the trailer started in the right direction."

Margy swings the wheel all the way to the right before she starts moving. The power steering squeals, and the rocks below the wheels squish. I know John hears this and is cringing in the background. He hates equipment abuse, no matter how minor.

The truck starts backwards, but Margy has turned too much, and the situation is getting rapidly worse. I yell at her to stop before the front of the trailer hits the rear of the truck. Bro is running around the front of the truck, getting in the way and adding to the tension. John has come forward to join Bob and me in our futile supervision.

"It's the J-word," I say to John and Bob. They both nod their heads.

Bob walks over to Margy's side of the truck, suggesting she pull straight ahead to avoid the developing jackknife. Then he calmly explains how to maneuver the truck into the best parking spot. Margy doesn't even hesitate. She pulls straight forward, straightens the trailer, and then backs the truck onto the road without missing a beat. She turns in the proper direction, following Bob's easy-going directions, and continues farther back until the truck and trailer are in-line. Then, under Bob's gentle guidance, she pulls forward. Her forward movement is precise, and she edges smoothly onto the shoulder in a near-perfect parking maneuver.

"Why does she listen to you, but never listens to me?" I kid Bob.

He laughs, puts on his jacket, and gets ready to ride.

As Margy and I off-load our quads, John and Bob point at the trailer from the other side of the road. John comes over and bends down by the trailer's wheel, and then reaches into the wheelwell behind the tire.

"This brake wire is jammed against the tire," he says. How did he see this from the other side of the road? Answer: He didn't see it at first, but he heard it rub as Margy pulled into the parking spot. Then he pointed it out to Bob from across the road. John constantly conducts preflight and postflight checks of every piece of equipment, never missing a thing.

"I'll push the wire back for now," John says. "But we'll need to get it fixed before the next trip."

"Maybe we should issue a manufacturer recall," I joke. There is only one trailer of this model in existence, a one-of-a-kind John-design.

Bob and John move their quads to the side of our trailer and put on their helmets. Margy is on her Honda, nearly ready to go. I'm still fumbling with my riding clothes, but I hop onto my Kodiak, knowing I am holding up the ride.

"Where's the starter button?" I quip. It has been a few weeks, but I'm not that forgetful.

Bob leans over from his Kodiak, thinking I am actually searching for the starter, and says: "On the bottom left – Wait a minute, yours is on the top left. My Kodiak is different. What's that bottom button?" As if I know.

"That's the override," say John, bailing me out. I'm granted a few minutes reprieve to get organized, as John and Bob launch into a technical discussion of the differences between my Kodiak and older models. I didn't even know I have an override button, nor do I have a hint about its purpose.

"Are you finally ready to go?" I say to Bob flippantly.

"Finally ready," answers Bob. He knows some babysitting is going to be necessary on this trip.

* * * * *

After the recent rains, the road is already dry, but there is no dust. It's one of the blessings of autumn rides. John leads, with Bob close behind, followed by Margy, and then me. As we ride, Bob pulls up parallel to John on the left side, and they carry on a nearly continuous conversation. How do they hear each other over the roar of the engines, especially with their helmets on? Sometimes John yells to me when we are positioned side-by-side, and I can hardly hear him. The conversation between Bob and John is simplified, because they have a good idea what the other is going to say. It's a lot like a pilot listening to air traffic control as ATC spits out a rapid-fire clearance. If you know what to expect, it's easy to hear the controller. If you are an airplane passenger without much flying experience, the clearance is verbal chaos.

Along the way, we pass two trucks, parked in separate turnouts. They are probably mushroom pickers. October is their month in the rain. Pine mushrooms and chanterelles are the ones that fetch the highest prices from mushroom buyers in town. This region is prime mushroom territory.

Riding along Haslam Lake, we come to the first bridge. It is in terrible shape. One of the crossbeams is broken, poking up at an awkward angle. This requires us to maneuver to the edge of the bridge to clear the protruding board. I watch Margy in front of me, as she smoothly slips past the broken beam. She has come a long way in dealing with her quad "altophobia" (*Up the Main*, Chapter 10). On this trip, John has proclaimed Goat 2 is a good test of her progress. Currently Margy's percentile score, as rated by John, is a comfortable 85. Of course, he won't accept anything less than 100.

This bridge is nearly trashed. But it is the next bridge, farther down the road, that is scheduled for demolition. Go figure. We cross the seemingly-solid second bridge, ignoring the new detour trail that is ready for use when the bridge is eventually taken out.

As we ride, Bob and John continue their side-by-side chat. I'm tempted to pull up next to Margy and try the same thing, but I know we won't be able to hear each other. Being comfortable with the riding environment is part of the secret. Margy and I are still so intent on our driving that we can't pay attention to anything else. John and Bob cruise on autopilot.

I smell smoke, and soon we pass a roadside slash with several piles of smoldering wood. These small, unattended fires set by the logging company seem dangerous when you first see them. But during rainy periods, there's little danger of the fire spreading. Still, it looks strange, knowing that no one has been here in hours. These slash-burns continue to smolder, clearing the land a little at a time.

We climb the hill at the north end of Haslam Lake and turn onto the new logging road. Or at least it was new a few months ago. The road is already worn down, but the trenches along the shoulders are still deep. We are able to increase our speed to 50 klicks on the relatively smooth surface. Around one corner, I am surprised to see a solo red quad sitting in a small turnout. The blond woman on the Grizzly looks tiny, as she sits kicked back on the big bike while reading a book. I catch a glimpse of a hunting rifle propped on the fender. We wave, and she waves back. Bob stops to talk to her, while we ride on.

When Bob catches up with us, we are on the downhill slope, headed towards Fiddlehead Farm. Bob pulls abreast of my quad and yells something over the roar of our engines. I hear a voice but no intelligible words. He shouts louder this time and then leans over and nearly yells in my ear. But with my helmet and the engine noise, I still don't understand. It sounds something like: "Late past light?"

"I don't speak English," I yell back at him. He nods and pulls forward to resume his conversation with John. (Later he tells me he simply asked: "How are you doing?" But after yelling a few times, he shouted: "Up late last night?" in deference to my inability to comprehend anything.)

We stop for a lunch break at Fiddlehead Farm. Then we ride along Rainbow Main, a road John knows is not active today. How does he know this?

Bro shifts side-to-side in his aft quad box, not barking, but obviously intent on something he has seen or smelled. After a while he settles back down, resting his chin on the box's edge, as we push along the fairly smooth road.

As we ease down a steep hill towards a bridge, John stops and waits for us to catch up. Intently, he inspects the logging slash on the side of the mountain directly ahead of us.

"Elk," says John. "Only one of them, and that's rare."

I stare and see nothing, but then the elk moves. Its tan body scrambles up the hill in leaps and bounds. We all see it now, but none of us would have spotted the elk if John had not called it to our attention.

"How'd you see it in all that clutter?" I ask.

"Got lucky this time," he replies. "You almost never see elk outside of a herd. But I was just looking in the right direction. Then it moved." Of course, John's eagle eyes help.

At the intersection with Goat Main, we pull to the side and wait. John clicks on his radio and sits feet-on-fenders.

"I smell diesel," says John. "A truck has been through here recently."

There is faint chatter on the radio, most of it brief and to the point. One truck calls from only a few miles away: "Downhill at 29, loaded." We strain to hear a truck thundering down Goat Main. In a few minutes, we hear the diesel approaching. A full load of logs passes our turnout, blasting through the intersection without even slowing.

Bob takes the radio and contacts the truck, briefly explaining our situation: "Truck departing the Rainbow intersection, we have four quads trying to make it to Goat Two. Is there anyone coming down the main behind you?"

"There's another load behind me, back a ways, but you should have time to make it to Goat Two," replies the logging truck driver. I notice he says "should."

We quickly crank up our bikes, and Bob makes a brief radio report before we pull onto the road: "Four quads up Goat Main from Rainbow to Goat Two."

We accelerate out onto Goat Main. Bob leads, and John follows faster than he normally cares to when carrying Bro. Margy and I bring up the rear. The road winds past the entrance to Goat 1 and then along the drop-off to Goat Lake. Margy doesn't slow a bit here. She should get at least two percentile points for keeping her throttle wide open.

Cliffs encroach the road now, and the bends are winding and blind. If a logging truck comes around the corner to meet us, it will be terribly exciting. I'm glad Bob and John are in the lead to face the ruckus first, if it occurs.

We round the final bend in close formation, and there is the turnoff to Goat 2. There are even road signs posted here. One (on the left) reads "Goat II," and the sign on the right proclaims "Goat 2." I guess you can call it whatever you want.

We stop at the turnoff, while Bob uses the radio to let the logging trucks know we are no longer on Goat Main: "Four quads at Goat Two, clear of the main."

Another sign, a bright red one near the "Goat 2" placard, reads: "Road Waterbarred." It's a formal way of saying "cross-trenched." As we rest for a few minutes before beginning the climb, a loaded logging truck thunders past, southbound.

'Missed us!" I yell defiantly as the truck roars down the main.

We start up the hill, and I take the opportunity to slip into second position behind John. I'm sure Bob will keep his eye on Margy, following behind me.

Huge reddish-brown and orange maple leaves cover the old road, with most of the yellow leaves still hanging on the branches. As we climb higher, alders soon replace the maples.

The trail becomes more challenging. Small waterfalls run right up to the road, crossing at the trenches. At one spot, there is a steep drop-off, with rocks aligned purposefully along the edge. As I pass, I look closer. I can see a washout has begun here, and the edge of the trail is gone, sliding steeply into the ravine below. My guess is John piled these rocks as a warning, during his visit earlier this week. This spot could be a challenge for a rider with altophobia.

I pull off to the inside edge of the trail, awaiting Margy's arrival. She passes me, glancing at the rock markers. But she barely slows down. This should be worth another percentile point. Bob passes me next, notices the rocks, and yells to me: "That's gonna go!" He's right, but I hope the erosion holds until we get back down Goat 2.

The climb continues through ever-deepening trenches, all filled with running water. I watch Bob approach a small tree that has fallen across the trail. He strategically spins his tires as he crosses over the trunk. He purposefully fishtails, to trim the limbs a bit. Bob looks back over his shoulder to inspect the results, and I raise an arm high in a motion of "Right on!"

On the climb out of one particularly steep trench, Margy delays her acceleration and gets stuck. She spins her wheels, and it gets worse. She turns to face me, and I yell: "Back up!" She does, but gets stuck again. Now there is no more room for her to back up, since she is in the trough of the trench. She rocks the bike a bit, trying to get moving. I get off my quad to lend a hand. Bob has backed up to assist too. It's almost winch time.

I reach Margy's bike just as she gives it another burst of throttle, and I push enough to get her going up the other side of the trench. Now she guns it. Mud and small rocks spurt from behind her tires, and all over me. She successfully makes it to the top. I'm not sure whether points should be added or deducted.

We pass through an area of old-growth trees. Many of these ancient cedars grow right next to the trail. Old-growth is sometimes left behind by the loggers, where the roots are necessary to stabilize the road.

We arrive at the stream which is the one where John tried to build up the rocky bottom to make a safer crossing. Two waterfalls merge to our left, flow across the trail, and exit down another steep slope to the right. Today, the creek flows more gently. Streams run differently day-to-day this time of year. Waterfalls sometimes disappear within hours after the rain stops. It's difficult to predict.

We cross the stream without any problems, push through an area of thick alders, and arrive at the end of the road. At least it is the end of the present-day road. We turn off our engines.

"Good job," John says specifically to Margy. "I'll give you an 88."

"Pretty generous, John," I say.

"She earned it. But I'll take back points if she starts to slip, so watch out." That'll keep her on her toes.

Bob was here 20 years ago as a logger, operating an A-frame from this location, dragging logs downhill to this spot on the old road. He points out a nearby stump with slash marks where the tower's cables were wrapped. A team of loggers worked this area with Bob, hauling the logs to trucks in a turnout that is still remarkably clear of vegetation.

"The road doesn't end here. It continues that way." Bob points straight ahead, and I can see traces of an old road. It's hard to believe nature has reclaimed this area so completely in 20 years. Another road, only slightly more visible, ran uphill to our left in those days. That's the road John wants to reactivate for our quads. It looks impossible.

After a snack, we push into the bush with our quads, following the old road upwards across a small trench. John and Bob lead. Margy and I stop only 50 feet into the bush, abandon our bikes, and walk behind the other two quads. Soon both John and Bob grind to a halt too, and we all start working our way up the old path on foot. We remove any boulders we can handle, and cut our way through the alders with pruning shears. After clearing this area, Bob and John drive a bit farther. Then they stop and work on the rocks and bushes some more. The going is rugged. I'm not sure how John and Bob will turn around when they are finished.

John grooms with finesse, using his clippers plus an eye for the slope of the terrain to determine the best route. Bob grooms with brute force, using his quad as a bulldozer, picking the quickest route. They work differently, tackling separate tasks, but the trail quickly takes shape as a single wandering path.

Meanwhile, Margy and I contribute some minor pruning of the branches along the trail. After a while, sweat permeates all three layers of my clothes. We walk in near-fog created by the cloud layer topping the ridges.

We continue to prune the bushes for almost a kilometer, and then Margy and I turn back, while John and Bob work on one final steep slope. We'll get an early start going down Goat 2, and still we expect John and Bob to catch up to us before we reach the bottom.

It is difficult to get our quads turned around at the spot where we left them. But finally we are past the end-of-road turnout and headed down the main trail. We enter the bottom of the cloud layer, and it begins to drizzle. In another 5 minutes, we are below the clouds completely, and a few minutes later the rain stops. The rest of the downhill ride is a visual joy, with waterfalls on both sides cascading down shear mountain walls. Not surprisingly, we reach the Goat 2 entrance turnout only a few minutes before Bob and John catch up with us.

* * * * *

On the ride back to our off-load spot, I bring up the rear. At one point, I notice Bob pulling up beside Margy, and he yells something at her. I can tell by Margy's shaking of her head that she doesn't hear him properly, and after a while he speeds forward to engage in an easier conversation with John. Bob rides side-by-side with John for several kilometers, talking and talking. When we come to an intersection, we stop our quads for a brief break. I ask Bob what he tried to tell Margy a few kilometers back.

"I asked if she was warm and dry?" says Bob. "But she couldn't hear me, I guess."

"I thought you said 'Do you know how to drive?'" says Margy.

We all laugh.

"She doesn't speak Canadian," I joke.

Further down the road, John comes to a sudden stop, and we all come to a halt around him. He gets off his bike and walks across the deep trench at the side of the road. He continues up the slope of the hill for another 50 feet, and then reaches down to retrieve something from the ground. At first, it looks to me like an orange piece of plastic, maybe a blasting cap. But it's a chanterelle mushroom. How John sees it that far from the road, while riding at 40 klicks, I'll never know.

"You hate mushrooms," I say.

"It's for Mom," says John. "She sometimes cuts them up real fine, and puts them in the pot with the meat. They're not too bad when I can't see them."

It's sort of like Bro's pills. You can grind them up and put them in his food, and he'll never know.

Chapter 15

Sliammon Detours

Chainsaws walk. Sometimes they walk real fast. It doesn't take long to realize you need to be careful where you place a running chainsaw. And I'm talking about a saw idling in neutral, without the chain turning. As the gasoline engine vibrates, chainsaws walk.

I know this, but sometimes I let my saw walk across the cabin's upper deck a few feet. I grab it just before it tumbles onto the lower deck. You just need to keep an eye on it. Better yet, place the chainsaw in a pile of wood to anchor it while you prepare the next piece for cutting.

One day, as I put the next log in the sawhorse, I momentarily place the chainsaw on the upper deck. I turn my back on the saw for only an instant, and it walks towards the edge of the deck. No, it runs! I turn just in time to see it flop over the side, onto the lower deck. Before I can get to it, the idling saw bounces off the lower deck, and kicks (a backflip!) into the water.

As the hot engine contacts the water, a spurt of smoky steam immediately rises. The engine stops instantly, and the saw begins to sink! But I am quick. I grab the saw by the chain end before it drops out of sight. Yes, I feel the sharp blades through my gloves. But there is no real danger to me – the chain froze the moment the engine quit. I haul the saw onto the lower deck. Only then, with the excitement over, do I yell a few choice obscenities regarding my stupidity.

I act quickly to disconnect the air filter and remove the spark plug. I pull the saw's starter rope through a few cycles, trying to clear the water from the combustion chamber. Then I replace the plug and filter and try to start the saw.

No surprise – the engine doesn't fire. I pull the spark plug out again and blow off any remaining moisture. I set the chainsaw on its side and pull the rope through. Then I place the saw in a sun-drenched spot, the spark plug hole pointing directly towards the sun. It's a bright February day, so things should dry fast. Every few minutes, using the starter rope, I pull the piston through again. I watch moisture puff from the spark plug hole. Maybe I can dry out the engine and get it started before I have to admit my stupidity to John.

No luck. Even after letting the saw sit overnight in the warm, dry cabin, I can't entice the engine to start. The cylinder fires briefly once, but it's only for an instant. It's time to see John, and confess.

* * * * *

The chainsaw sits in front of John. Obviously, I've brought it to town because of a problem. I try to break it to him gently.

"I can't get it started," I moan. "It got wet."

"Wet? How wet?" John sees right through me.

"Well, it fell into the water."

"Not good. How did you get it out?" The water surrounding my cabin is deep on all sides, even near the shore where the cliffs descend nearly straight down into the lake.

"I grabbed it by the chain, just as it started to sink. The bad part is it was running when it went into the water. It stopped real quick, giving off some ugly smoke. I hope I didn't shock cool it."

· "Oh." That's all that John says. I expect more. He pauses, then continues: "They're tough little machines," says John. "We should be able to get 'er runnin' again. Did you check the plug?"

"I dried it off and pulled the starter through a lot of times with the plug removed. Could water still be somewhere inside?"

"It's usually the plug," says John. "You were lucky. How'd you drop it into the water?" It's time to face the music.

"I set it down and turned my back for just a minute. It walked off the deck."

"Leave it here, and I'll take a look tonight. You gotta watch where you put a saw down. They'll run away from you real quick."

That's all. No lecture, just a reminder. But I'm sure my chainsaw's engine is destroyed.

* * * * *

To my surprise, John gets the saw running by merely drying and cleaning the spark plug. I thought I had properly cleaned the plug by blowing on it and letting it dry overnight.

"Here's something that works good for cleaning a plug," says John, as he pulls a cigarette lighter out of his pocket and flicks it on. "It gets rid of all the gunk on the tip." John carries a lighter he found on the trail in Theodosia. He doesn't smoke, but this lighter is one of his favorite multi-purpose tools.

I'm back in business, and pleased it has been that easy. I put the chainsaw in Margy's truck, ready to haul back to the cabin.

* * * * *

When Margy and I ride without John, we need to remember how he takes care of us in every respect. Today, as we head north on Highway 101, we receive our first reminder.

"We forgot to get gas for the quads," says Margy, with surprise in her voice. You'd think we'd at least remember something that basic. But, no, here we are nearly out of town, and no gas. It's amazing we're able to do anything without John.

"Oops. We can stop at the Wildwood store," I offer.

Of course, in all of our riding, we've only gotten gas at two gas stations in town. But we ought to be able to handle a different gas station in Wildwood without John.

Margy maneuvers her truck up to the pumps near the store. They even have marine fuel, so she pulls up to that pump. The sign reads: "Full Serve," but I assume that doesn't apply to quads. As I climb onto the trailer, the female attendant steps out of the office door. She hands me the hose to the marine pump.

"Double trouble," she notes, looking at our long trailer, carrying our two quads.

"That's us," I reply.

"Where to?" she asks.

"Up Wilde Road, maybe all the way to Chippewa Lake"

"Could be some downed trees," she responds. "Lots of wind with last night's storm." This is my first hint, but I ignore it.

As we pull back onto the highway, I notice what else is missing besides the gas. I reach into my backpack and extract my sunglasses. There hasn't been a reason to wear them for weeks.

"There, that's better," I say, as I turn to model my sunglasses for Margy. "Now I'm ready for anything."

We turn off the highway at Wilde Road and continue another kilometer. Margy backs the trailer into the turnout trail that John has shown us. It's a nice open area to off-load our quads. Our plan today is to ride the dirt logging road uphill towards the Bunster Range as far as we can go in the snow. Then we'll pull off to the side, so others can pass, and snowshoe up the trail from there. I expect we'll be able to make it to the Chippewa Lake turnoff before we are into the snow. Then we can decide whether to stay on the main trail or try the climb up to the lake.

We fasten our snowshoes and poles to the front racks of our quads with bungee straps, change into our rain gear, and begin the climb. Right away, we encounter scattered branches on the road, not surprising considering the previous night's severe wind. For a brief moment, I recall the gas station attendant's warning. I also remember the chainsaw in the back of the truck, awaiting transport to our cabin. When off-roading, John always carries his saw. Today we are going up a trail without him, right after the passage of a major storm. Yet, my freshly-tuned chainsaw sits in the truck a kilometer behind us. For that brief instant, I consider turning back to retrieve the saw. But I don't.

We pass the sign that announces: "Warning – Road Deactivated." Almost immediately, we see the significant aftermath of the storm. A log has fallen across the road, and I stop to inspect it. It's small, so I decide we can easily cross it. I drive my quad over it, and Margy follows. No problem. But if I had my chainsaw, I could have cleared the road for others, like John always does.

Within another half-kilometer, a larger log is tilted over the road. We won't be able to drive over this one. Fortunately, thick branches on the left side of the road brace the fallen log. We are able to duck low and drive under. I know our luck can't last. And there sits the chainsaw, in the truck, now far behind us.

We pass the Sliammon Lake turnoff. The lake's access road looks like a muddy mess. Even in good summer conditions, it is a rough road for a conventional motor vehicle, but it's usually easy for a quad. We continue up the main, across Appleton Creek, where the water roars by fast today. Within a hundred meters, we are stopped dead by a one-foot log blocking the trail. It has fallen at an odd angle, suspended a few feet above the ground by it's own branches. Too high to ride over, and too low to slip under. I get off my quad to look closer. There is no way to get past this obstacle. It's time to turn back. And we haven't even reached the snow.

We reverse course, now headed back down the main. This is a good excuse to try some of the side trails that drop off the road on either side. The first one we pick is an interesting challenge. It leads off to the left, winding through muddy terrain, with the expected challenges of more fallen logs. But we navigate these obstacles by driving over them or motoring to the side of the trail, to pass under the hanging branches. In one case, an otherwise no-go small log lies too high to go over and too low to slip under. But it is light, rotted wood. So I get off my quad and easily heave it to the side. The old log collapses upon itself, with a loud "Crack!"

At one muddy crossing, the water extends farther ahead than I able to see. A creek enters from the left and follows the trail around the bend. The bottom of the diverted stream is barely visible, so I proceed slowly to make sure the depth is acceptable. The water comes up to my running boards in places, but we make it through without getting stuck.

After the first few kilometers, the trail winds uphill so dramatically I wonder if we may have found a path to the snow. Then the path deteriorates fast, rushes up a steep slope, and ends in a hodgepodge of logs and branches. I get off my quad and climb over the obstacles. The route is completely impassible beyond, at least without a chainsaw.

We take a snack break before starting back down. On the way out, Margy leads. After a few hundred meters, she gets stuck in the bottom of a moderate trench, her quad wedged between a boulder and the steep slope behind her. I watch Margy try to maneuver out of the ditch by backing up, but her bike is no match for the situation. I get off my quad to assist, figuring I can push her front wheels to the side of the rock. First, I decide to see if I can budge the boulder instead. It rolls easily to the side, and we're on our way again.

Back on the main road, we continue down towards Sliammon Lake, trying a few side trails that go nowhere, just dead ends. As we approach the Sliammon cutoff, a white van with its lights on is parked at the entrance. In the van, a woman is reading a book or maybe a map. I wave to her, she waves back, and we continue down the entry road. I wonder if we should have stopped and asked if she needs help. I doubt she is lost at such an obvious intersection, but we could have at least offered assistance. Now the van is behind us. We will be staying only briefly at the lake. If the woman is still parked at the entry when we return, I'll be sure to stop and talk with her.

The road down to the lake is a mess. It's easily navigable, but it's so rutted and flooded that I wonder how it will be usable for standard vehicles when summer arrives.

At the lake, we stop only a few minutes. Then we restart our engines and begin to maneuver for turnaround. As I back to the side of the road, a red canoe appears from between the trees near the shore. It heads for the boat pullout area. In the front of the canoe is a huge stack of shiny green salal. A tall, youthful fellow is barely visible at the stern of the canoe, seemingly encased within the mass of leaves. I wave to him, and he waves back. Then I complete my turnaround and watch Margy do the same.

Similar to when I observed the van, I wonder if we should offer assistance. There is no vehicle here at the shore, so could this fellow be hauling his salal harvest out of the area on-foot?

This time, I turn back without further hesitation. By now, the lad has already stowed the canoe. He is busy arranging two large bundles of salal.

"Do you have a vehicle?" I yell over my engine.

"A van is waiting for me at the entrance," he says. "The road is too rough to get down here today."

"Can I carry the salal out for you?" I ask. "Maybe we can strap it to my rear box."

"Sure, let's do that," he replies. "We can put a pile on the front and one on the back, if that's okay with you."

His salal is already tied with rope into two piles, each over a meter high. Margy is waiting for me around the corner, so...

"We can give you a ride too," I say. "You can load one pile on the other quad, and then hop on the back with me." Margy's quad can handle a light load, but her bike is too small for doubling with a passenger.

"No problem. I'll just carry a pile on my head. Salal pickers are used to doing that."

I laugh as I try to find a better position to hold onto the pile already heaped on my front rack. I can drive slowly with my right hand, thumb on the throttle, while using my left arm to secure the salal. The young fellow hops aboard behind me, with the second pile of salal balanced on his shoulders and the back of his neck, held tight by his lanky arm.

"Ready!" he yells, acting like he travels this way every day.

Up we go on the rutty road. My concentration is on the trail, trying to keep my uphill momentum going, but not so fast as to lose my grip on the salal. I'm trying to steer with one hand. I feel a hand on my helmet, as the salal picker balances his load. I glance back and notice the salal is not really on his head but on the back of his shoulders, protruding upward and out. It looks like some kind of giant fan-shaped hat. He returns my glance with an enormous grin. I wish I had a picture of this.

At the entry intersection, the young man hops off before I am at a complete stop. He grabs the salal pile from the front rack, and somehow finds a free hand to open the rear door of the van. He tosses both piles of salal into the van nearly simultaneously and yells "Thanks!" The woman in the van puts down her book and throws me a pleasant smile.

I am back on the road so quickly that Margy doesn't even have to stop as she approaches the intersection. Salal hauling mission complete.

We continue down the road, briefly exploring other trails on both sides. Each quickly terminates in a dead end. When we are less than a half-kilometer from our truck, I catch a glimpse of another prospective trail jutting off to the left. It passes by too rapidly to stop in time, so I do a U-turn in the road and head back. Margy follows.

This trail proves to be the highlight of the day. It winds through a thickly forested region, going nearly constantly downhill. The path has been meticulously groomed, although it does not appear to have been used in recent days. It is barely wide enough for a quad. In several places, I need to drive very slowly to prevent the snowshoe poles on my front rack from hitting trees at either side of the trail. Someone has paid a lot of attention to the maintenance of this trail. It's perfectly sized and groomed for quads.

One final steep downhill slope ends at a widened area at the approach to a long wooden bridge. The shake-block bridge crosses Sliammon Creek, below the lake. The water is running winter-wild today. The 100-foot bridge looks barely sturdy enough to walk on, saying nothing of crossing it on a quad.

The scene is simultaneously tranquil and violent. The creek is running at near-capacity, water tumbling below the bridge in a series of small waterfalls crossing a jumble of jammed logs. On the opposite side of the creek, a back-eddy spews a mass of foamy bubbles under a huge moss-covered maple tree at the water's edge. Drooping branches nearly drag the water. It is a rainforest scene of rugged beauty, wet and cold.

I walk out onto the bridge, checking its condition. I wish John could advise me. He would know if it is safe to continue across on a quad. The wood seems weak in the center, but a quad's tires would straddle the bridge's support beams which run alongside the edges. I think it might be safe, but I am not ready to test it today.

As I look across the bridge to the opposite shore, I am satisfied for today's ride to end here. But maybe another day, with John along...

Chapter 16

Winter Ride

It's a temptation – our quads are already loaded on the trailer, and the truck is hooked up, ready to go. Margy and I returned our quads to the hangar after a day at the mall's bookstore, and that's where the truck and trailer now sit. The two red machines were used as visual aids at the mall, to draw attention to my book promotional display. It provoked interest in the books, but the most common question of the day was: "How much are the raffle tickets?" It's a common sight to see quads in the mall, being raffled off by one of the local non-profit organizations. We aren't licensed to raffle quads, nor would we sell our trusty machines. But the obvious interest in quad raffle tickets is an alluring idea.

The bigger temptation tonight is totally different. The quads are ready to go, and the truck is connected. Why not leave both the trailer and truck in the airport hangar, ready to ride the next day? Good question, but there is a valid answer: it's mid-December, and the weather has been wet and cold.

Margy and I give into the enticement and leave her truck hitched to the trailer, sticking out of the front of the hangar. We drive back to the condo in my white Ford Tempo, sporting its big yellow banana (kayak) on top. We'll be ready to go riding in the morning.

I telephone John to see if he wants to join us. For a change, I hope the answer is "No," since this is not the kind of ride he would enjoy. It will need to be short because of the brief span of winter daylight. We plan to travel up the lake in the Campion after the trail ride (and before darkness falls), so this trip will require a near-dawn departure. Neither short rides nor early mornings sit well with John.

"It'll be short, but we haven't ridden in weeks," I explain. "We'd love for you to join us, but we'll need to be back in town by two o'clock."

"That's not much of a ride," replies John. "Besides, I've promised Doug we'll go up to the A-Branch ski cabin. You'd like that better."

"We couldn't make it back from the ski cabin by two o'clock."

"No." Canadian long drawn-out. "Where are you planning to go?" In other words, it's impossible to ride anywhere worthwhile on such a compressed schedule.

"Can't go far," I concur. "So I thought we'd keep it simple. We can park where we off-loaded when I went with you to the Eldred River. Then we can ride up Goat Main, at least as far as Windsor Lake."

The Eldred River trip was over three months ago, but John remembers details. He'll remember where we parked to off-load the quads.

"Even then, you'll need to get started early," he reminds me. I doubt John has any regrets he is going to A-Branch rather than on a boring drive on Goat Main.

"Remind me about the parking area – the one with the parallel spur," I inquire.

I hope John doesn't remember how long he had to wait for me at this spot at the end of the trip to the Eldred River. That day, I lagged behind on the return trip, poking around at Dodd Lake. When I called him on the walkie-talkie to tell him I was delayed, he demanded a reason. John doesn't consider a trip complete until everyone is accounted for back at the parking area. My truthful reason for the delay: "I'm slow." That never pleases John. When I finally arrived back at the parking spot, John barely waved, as he quickly sped away in his truck.

"It's only a few miles up Goat Main from Tin Hat Junction," instructs John. "You can't miss it, on the right. If you don't see it until it's too late to stop, you can make the next right turn to loop back and park."

"Is it beyond where you'll turn off for A-Branch?" I ask.

"Quite a bit beyond – I'll turn off at Tin Hat Junction. That's if I go at all. I've been up A-Branch a lot lately, and it's getting old. Besides, Brody is pretty tired from yesterday's ride to Theo."

If John has promised Doug, there's no way he'll let him down. He is going to A-Branch.

"Hey, John," I say just before hanging up. "One of the front tires on Margy's quad is low. I need to ask you a stupid question."

John is used to my stupid questions. When we pushed the quad into the mall, I noted the soft tire, but my mechanical ability is just short of zero.

"Can I use an air hose at a gas station for a quad tire?" I ask. Now there's a stupid question.

I carry an electric air pump that can be connected to the quad's DC receptacle, but I've only used it once (under John's supervision). John insists I carry all the right tools, but I'm not sure what to do with most of them.

"Sure, just use the same hose you use for your car," he says. "There's a tire pressure gauge under the seat of Margy's quad." John knows our equipment better than we do.

"Okay, I know the pressure is only 4 PSI, but should I worry about the tire? I'm not sure why it's low." I don't want any problems on one of our first without-John trips into the backcountry.

"No, it's probably just one of those things, unless you see a gash," he replies. "Rick is always adding air to his tires." I don't think to ask why Rick needs air and John doesn't. "It keeps coming out all of the time," he adds.

Sometimes things John says don't make sense to me, but if John says it, then it's true. I'm satisfied, and I'll be ready to go in the morning. Of course, a short jaunt up Goat Main isn't exactly a voyage into what John would call the wilderness.

* * * * *

It takes an alarm to get me out of bed. In mid-December, if you wait until dawn, you'll be sleeping until 8 o'clock.

We drive the Tempo from the condo to the airport. With the truck already connected to the trailer, it's a fast departure from there. The weather is cooperating wonderfully, with only patches of morning fog and lots of blue sky above.

On the way out of town, Margy pulls into the gas station, and we fill our quads with marine gas. I use the air hose to inflate Margy's front tire. Sure enough, the tire gauge is under the seat, right where John said it was.

As I pump the air, it dawns on me why Rick inflates his tires so often. These low-pressure tires are more rubber than air. They take the jolts well. But if you hit a quad tire hard, it can momentarily separate from the rim and lose air. I remember John demonstrating this on one of the tires he and Rick purchased at a bargain price. The brothers jacked up both of their quads in the carport, replaced all eight tires, and pumped them up. Then John pushed with his hand on the sidewall of one of the tires. I could hear the air gushing out. John and Rick decided to return the tires for a refund. You don't get away with anything where these brothers are concerned.

The other part of the equation is the way Rick drives. He is a very experienced rider, but drives hard, whacking his tires to airless oblivion. John, on the other hand, carries Brody in his aft-box seat. So he rides slower and gentler through the rough terrain. As inexperienced riders, Margy and I ride slower and gentler too. But you can still bash a tire hard on a rock or stump. Just in case, I carry (because John says so) a spray can of tire repair foam and a complete tire repair kit, as well as the electric pump. But I'd prefer to use these only under John's supervision.

After leaving the gas station, we continue down Highway 101 to Dixon Road. We merge with Goat Main at the one-way loop. As we continue up the main, fog comes and goes in patches that hover over the logging slashes. Margy is traveling at a moderate and safe speed on the dirt road. But I wonder if it is too much for the trailer. I glance back through the covered cab. The trailer seems to be riding well over the potholes. Yet, I also know Margy's truck rides smooth, while the trailer is not nearly as well insulated from the bumps. The comfort of the truck can cover up the bouncing of the trailer behind us.

I consider suggesting she drive slower, but I'm afraid that will result in a speed slower than slow. When riding with Margy, I don't ever remember suggesting she slow down.

We pass the sign that captivated me the first time I saw it: "Up the Main from Tin Hat." It's a VHF radio call location for logging trucks traveling up Goat Main. We pass the intersection called Tin Hat Junction, a name which makes no sense to me. We are still on Goat Main and several kilometers south of where Tin Hat Road actually splits off towards Tin Hat Mountain. But it's even labeled on the map as Tin Hat Junction, so that's that.

In the remaining few miles, the shoulders of the road become edged with snow. We have climbed gradually from the highway, and now the snow suddenly appears. It is only a few inches deep, and the road itself remains dry. But the abrupt appearance of the snow is a bit of a surprise. The temperature is now a few degrees above zero (Celsius), and there has been no significant precipitation for several days.

We easily identify the off-load spot. We slow in time to catch the spur that leads to the parking area, so the entry is uncomplicated. Margy pulls clear of the road in a wide area where we can leave our ramps down while we are riding. It's a nice luxury to return to the trailer after a ride and drive right up onto the ramps.

We start the quads' engines and wait for them to warm up, which takes awhile in the winter. Meanwhile, we begin to remove the tie-down straps. My Kodiak is missing a strap; yet, we know we tightly secured all of them this morning. Additionally, my quad has shifted on the trailer, to the right side with the front wheel wedged against the guardrail. It is difficult to imagine how my bike could have moved with enough force to throw a strap. On the way home, I will remind Margy to slow down, even if that means an overcorrection and a slow creep down the main.

I remember a more dramatic incident involving a loose quad. John and his nephew were traveling on a logging road, with John's Grizzly in the back of his truck and Chris' Kodiak on a trailer towed behind them. As they climbed a small hill, John hit a pothole. He glanced in his rearview mirror, and Chris' quad was gone! John quickly pulled over to the shoulder, and they ran back down the hill to find the Kodiak sitting in the middle of the road. It must have been quite a jolt, coupled with the incline, to toss the quad off the trailer. The Kodiak sat dead-center in the road, its gearshift still in "Park."

It takes a few minutes to don our winter clothes. I'm already wearing long johns and lined nylon pants. Three layers of shirts cover me, including a heavy red and gold University of Southern California sweatshirt. I'm wearing the shirt in celebration of Reggie Bush winning the Heisman Trophy the evening before (forever a USC football fan!). I pull on an outer pair of rain pants and my heavy-lined jacket. My head and face will be toasty under my black, full-face ski mask, with holes for my eyes and nose. Along with the thermal protection from my helmet and goggles, my face should stay plenty warm.

My hands will be the weak link today. My gloves are water ski gloves that work fine in the summer, but are not nearly thick enough for December. Where did my heavy gloves go? Then again, how cold can it get in the winter sun? Answer: at any speed above 30 klicks, bone chilling.

I'm also missing other equipment besides gloves: my GPS, satellite phone and the walkie-talkies. These are items I like to carry when riding. We came to town for the book sale at the mall, and these items were left behind at the cabin. I failed to consider the fact that good weather quickly prompts me to go riding, hiking, or kayaking. It's an often-repeated pattern of omission, and I make a mental note to put together a go-to-town bag to prevent this from happening in the future.

As we climb out of the snow-covered off-load area, the airflow over our quads pushes the wind chill temperature well below zero. My fingers quickly get cold. Chilly air pushes up under my jacket sleeves too, and I struggle to slip my cuffs down. This necessitates release of the thumb-activated throttle to adjust my cuff. Awkwardly, I readjust my jacket as I ride. Occasionally, I remove a hand from the handlebars and clench my fist for warmth, a process that is most difficult for my throttle hand.

Margy leads, and I wonder if she is encountering these same challenges. My guess is she thought ahead more than me. I noticed she donned thick gloves and probably adjusted her jacket with more finesse. She attends to such details more efficiently than I do.

Within less than a kilometer, Tin Hat Road splits to the left of Goat Main (the real Tin Hat Junction). We remain on Goat Main, following it north. The air is noticeably warmer now. The higher we climb, the warmer it gets. That's backwards, of course. Our parking area must be in a spot where the dense cold air sinks and collects.

As we continue up the main, sunny skies alternate with foggy patches. The foggy areas lie over the logging slashes and along the lake shoreline to our right. The snow along the road's edge is almost gone, and my fingers are tolerably cold.

I accelerate around Margy, and then slow down again to 45 klicks. This is a comfortable speed on a main road, and barely acceptable for the chill factor today. I feel the winter air pushing against my chest through four layers of clothing. It is a biting blast of cold. My fingers burn a bit, but I know it is far from frostbite. So I just complain to myself. I now understand John's justification for installing electric heaters on his quad: handgrip warmers and a thumb-throttle heater. I'll laugh at him no more.

Entering the foggy patches, I slow down a little. The visibility remains adequate to see and avoid traffic coming the other way. We ride with our lights on, for an added level of comfort. See and be seen.

The Dodd Lake turn-off comes up faster than I expect. Rather than take the turn at too fast a speed, I slow gradually, passing the main entrance before I stop. Just past the entry, I slip down a quad-sized incline that rejoins the Dodd turn-off. Margy follows, though she slows more than necessary. She barely creeps down the slope. I'm glad she takes the challenge of the incline, rather than doing a U-turn to use the main entrance. But her slow crawl downward tells me she feels uncomfortable with the steepness of this path.

At the lake, we park and stretch in the winter sun. The lake itself is partially shrouded in fog, providing a surreal landscape as seen from the shore. Dodd Lake is not typically overrun with people, even in the summer. On this December day, there is absolutely no one at the lake, except us.

Departing the lakeside parking area, I lead us through the campsites and then back out the same way we entered. It is not necessary to take the narrow inclined path this time, but it is more challenging. So I drive up the steep shortcut again and out onto Goat Main.

I park on the main to await Margy. She begins to follow, powers forward only a few feet up the incline, and stops. She backs down carefully, and then uses the main entrance spur to rejoin the road. When she comes around the corner to my parked location, I yell at her: "Wimp!" She probably can't hear me through her helmet and over the sound of our engines. But she gets the meaning and gives me a disgusted shrug.

Continuing up Goat Main from Dodd Lake, my goggles fog around the edges. I lower them over my helmet's protruding mouthguard so I can see better. The air is warmer now, but the wind chill is still significant at 45 klicks. Without goggles, the biting cold enters my helmet, pushes into my ski mask, and flows down my neck. The cold blast forces tears from my eyes. In a few kilometers, my goggles are clear again, so I pull them back up and over my eyes. My face is a lot warmer.

The turn-off at Windsor Lake is wide. It provides a glimpse of majestic scenery: a shimmering lake with scattered clouds against snow-capped mountains.

We pause for lunch, and then investigate a wooden pontoon-shaped hulk on the shore. It is constructed of carved cedar logs with metal-covered runners. Thick, rusty cables lash the barge-like vehicle together. It is obviously very old and of heavy-duty construction. I'll consult John regarding this hulk – he'll know its use and history. The structure should float, but what about those metal runners? Why would they be necessary on a lake that seems too deep to freeze?

Later, John has an explanation, and it doesn't involve a barge. This "sled" carried a steam donkey that winched itself through the forest over a skid road made of cedar planks. Then the sled was secured to the trees, allowing the donkey to winch logs to the pickup area and haul them back down to the lake. After the logging was finished, the pontoon-shaped sled was discarded in Windsor Lake. During the recent leveling project at the turnout area, forestry workers found the old hulk and hauled it onto shore. Here at Windsor Lake, it serves as a preserved yet unlabeled chunk of logging history.

Margy leads the way back to the truck. There is still one necessary stop. As we approach Dodd Lake, I pull in front of Margy, speeding ahead enough to be sure I am in position when she reaches the lake's entry road. I pull off the main at the steep path that won the battle with Margy earlier. When she comes around the corner far enough to see me, I drive down the steep slope that she would not climb a few hours ago. Margy follows me down.

At the bottom of the narrow incline, I turn around and pause for a moment so she understands my intensions. Then I push my quad's thumb-throttle forward and power up the steep path and out onto Goat Main.

Without hesitation, Margy positions her quad squarely in-line with the bottom of the steep trail. Then she guns it, and climbs up the incline and out onto the main.

When she stops on the road, I raise my fist in triumph: "Right on!"

Inside her helmet, and out of my sight, I'm certain there's a well-deserved smile.

Chapter 17

In Like a Lion

M arch comes in like a lion and goes out like a lamb. Or so they say. So far, only one week into the month, March is particularly rough. It's been nearly continual rain and wind. Today, Margy and I have an evening appointment in town. Weather permitting, we plan to go down the lake in the late afternoon.

The morning is blustery. When the Hole gets this windy, it's always a mess on the lower lake. Only one other nearby cabin, in the back of the Hole, is occupied today. Overnighters other than us are rare on the lake in the winter, and those who do stay make their visits brief. Meanwhile, we chug along with nearly continuous occupancy at Number 3, riding out the winter storms.

The late-morning wind whips strong enough to spin the blades of the wind generator ("We're making electricity!"). I'm surprised to see *Private Dancer*, the green and white boat from the other occupied cabin, plowing out of the Hole. It proceeds slowly through the rare conditon of whitecaps in this bay. *Private Dancer* enters the channel, and turns south towards First Narrows. I wouldn't chance a departure with winds like this, but this boater is probably more experienced. Yet, his slow pace indicates caution. If the North Sea is too rough, he can always turn back.

Sure enough, fifteen minutes later, *Private Dancer* returns. Good decision.

By noon, the winds have eased considerably. *Private Dancer* pokes her bow out again, and this time does not return.

The marine forecast indicates decreasing winds in the early evening, after passage of the cold front. We elect to wait until near sunset before departing for town. I don't want to race darkness down the lake, but a later departure should provide a reduction in wind, at least if you believe the forecast. Then again, as a pilot, I'm familiar with the power of cold fronts. They are narrow, fast moving weather systems, with abrupt wind shifts at the frontal boundary. Sometimes an energetic squall line precedes the passage of the front. So it's worth paying attention to the marine weather reports. Without TV or Internet weather charts to rely on, radio reports best document the conditions.

We're packed and ready to go at 3:30, but I'd prefer to wait for the 4 PM marine forecast. There will be updates of the ocean buoy weather data and an automated report from Grief Point at Powell River. The last hour's report showed Sentry Shoals with winds at 35 knots and gusting. Grief Point reported 28 knots from the southeast, with gusts to 35. As good as the conditions are in the Hole, these reports bode problems on the lower lake.

At 4:10, the new marine forecast for the Strait of Georgia is issued. There is no change in the projections from the previous report. That's a good sign – things are not going downhill. Grief Point's latest automated report is 25 knots from the east, with gusts to 35. The Queen of Burnaby makes a mid-strait report: southeast winds at 30 knots, with 5-foot swells. Even this large ferry is rocking-and-rolling today.

All looks okay for our departure, although I am suspicious. Frontal passage has not yet occurred. The expected wind shift to the west has not been reported anywhere in the Strait of Georgia. I don't want to be caught on the lake just as the front passes.

We launch from Cabin Number 3 with a self-promise that we will return if it is too rough – *Private Dancer* demonstrated a reassuring lesson. Tonight's appointment in town is not essential. Weather on this lake can far exceed my abilities, as well as push the limitations of the Campion.

Surprise! The North Sea is nearly calm, and it's brightening to the south. The clouds over Powell River are dark, but here and there the sun breaks through. Still, I crowd the east shoreline, knowing that John's Cabin Number 1 is a safe haven if the lake gets rough.

Southward we travel, the throttle reduced slightly to lessen the slap of small waves against the hull. I glance at my watch – it's 4:45. We'll be at the Shinglemill by 5:00, unless the waves intensify and we have to slow down further. That will put us in town before dark. We've got it made.

As I point the nose of the Campion into its docking berth, a gust reminds me that conditions are still unstable. This boat handles well in blustery situations, and we slide in against the dock in an almost-perfect arrival. The trip down the lake has been remarkably unexciting. But where is that cold front?

It takes a few minutes to unload the boat and leave the parking lot. At 5:15, we make the left turn onto Highway 101. Devastation from the storm is evident everywhere!

Branches lie all over the road. Rounding the corner at the townsite, I get my first view of the chuck. Near the paper mill, large swells catch the last rays of the setting sun. These waves are huge! All the way into town, the road is covered with tree limbs. We have obviously just missed a really big storm. But how did we miss it? The town has been ravaged. Yet, on the lake, nothing.

Later, I learn that a Piper Navajo aircraft crashed at Powell River Airport at 4:45 PM, killing the co-pilot. The twin-engine airplane conducted a missed approach on the first landing attempt. Then, on the second attempt, the aircraft landed downwind in a swirling gust, as the wind shifted abruptly from east to west. The time of the crash coincided almost exactly with the moment we passed John's Cabin Number 1 in conditions of light wind and moderate chop. The cold front must have pounded Powell River hard, losing its punch as it moved inland. Somehow, the blast slipped just south of our position. Still, how could we have missed the whole thing? More significantly, how did such a violent storm miss us?

We arrive at our condo just in time for the 6 PM Vancouver TV news. The lead story is about a savage storm that ripped through Powell River just before 5 PM. The freakish winds were blamed for the fatal airplane crash at the local airport. Sailings of both of Powell River's ferries (Comox and Texada Island) were cancelled, with peak winds of 109 kilometers per hour reported at the height of the blow. Except for the branches strewn all over the road, we missed the whole thing.

* * * * *

With the freak storm behind us, the weather turns cold. Snow falls on-and-off for two days. Then the sun returns for the weekend. It's just in time to go for a ride and snowshoe hike with John.

Margy and I arise early on Saturday morning, drive to the airport, and hook up to the quad trailer. Ahead of schedule for a change, we park in the Westview Marina parking lot, where there are double spaces for vehicles with trailers. We're always holding John up, so today we'll be ready! We get ahead of things by donning our riding clothing and preflighting the quads in the parking lot. While Margy fights with her boots and rain pants, a Canadian Coast Guard crewman stops by to admire our quads.

"Nice day for riding," he says, looking over our quads.

"Personally, I'd rather be out in your boat," I remark. The 47-foot *Cape Caution* has recently replaced the *Mallard*, an older Coast Guard ship. The new all-weather cutter sports a high-tech bridge and is both self-righting and self-bailing. The ship is supposedly capable of turning completely over, a full 360 degree roll, without taking on water.

"You wouldn't have wanted to be out there on Wednesday," notes the crewman. "That was a wild storm, and we were plenty busy with all sorts of rescue calls."

"We missed that storm," I reply, figuring it would be difficult to explain how we missed this wild blow. "Were you in the *Cape Caution* that day?"

"No, I was in the inflatable boat," he replies. "It's actually a better place to be in bad weather than the ship." I can believe it. The inflatable is powered by two monster outboards. I often watch the Coast Guard from the balcony of our condo, as they pound big waves in this impressive lifeboat.

"Looks like a better day today," I remark. "We haven't seen real sunshine in almost two weeks.

"It's gonna be a beauty," he says. "Have a good one."

As the crewman walks toward the marina, I ponder what a great place this is. It's not unusual to have a morning conversation with the Coast Guard in the parking lot, as we both begin a day of personal adventure.

* * * * *

The snowshoes are my idea. Margy goes along with the concept, though I'm sure she remembers our previous expeditions. Those treks were demanding. On one trip in marginal snow conditions, hiking boots would have been more efficient than snowshoes. Walking in snowshoes, lifting the contraptions high above the snow and swinging each foot forward, is a major effort.

John knows snowshoes a lot better than we do, and he isn't a big fan. On previous snowy hikes, I've watched him stride, seemingly effortlessly, on snowshoes. His large, old-style wooden snowshoes carry him almost twice as fast as my modern-design aluminum shoes. And John doesn't use poles. Without poles, I'd be helpless.

"Maybe I'll give it a try," says John, as he loads his snowshoes into his truck. I know he won't merely park his quad and watch us wander off into the snow alone. Already, in his normal intricate detail, John has a route planned out. We will start in Theodosia Valley and then branch off to Heather Main for the climb up to the snow.

It's evident John is in a hurry-up mode today. It's hard to keep up with him under routine conditions, but when he is in a rush, it's like trying to follow lightning. Using the extra time at the marina parking lot to get organized proves wise. Margy and I are already nearly fully dressed for the cold. Our snowshoes and poles are strapped together and ready to load, and our riding gear is organized and loaded in our quad storage boxes.

At the gas station, we fill up the three quads with marine fuel and top-off both trucks. John is anxious to leave the station. I ask if I can ride with him.

"Sure," he says. "But the cab is a mess."

"Don't move a thing. I can find room," I reply. Easier said than done. The truck seat is crowded with John's helmet, tools, a pile of heavy clothes, a thick maintenance manual for his quad, and Bro. I push the clothes and manual to the side underneath Bro, put the tools on the floor, and place the helmet on my lap. Still it's a tight squeeze.

We're out of the gas station so fast that I wonder if Margy will be able to follow us. But John always keeps her in his rear view mirror when we travel together, and Margy knows our planned turnoff from the highway. So I hang on, as we rumble out of town.

When we pull off Highway 101 onto Southview Road, John says he doesn't see Margy behind us.

"When did you lose her?" I ask.

"Haven't seen her since the gas station," says John matter-of-factly. "She might have gotten tied up in traffic at that first stoplight." This isn't like John, even in his hurry-up mode.

We wait at the intersection for a few minutes until Margy's arrives. Then John leads our two-truck caravan for a few kilometers, to a wide turnoff on a curve where there's lots of snow already on the ground. Margy should be able to pull completely off the road here with the trailer. We get out of John's truck, as Margy appears around the curve.

"She can turn the trailer around here, and you'll be pointed back down the road," says John, knowing Margy is going to find the turn-around a challenge.

In a wide-swinging arm gesture, John motions to Margy: turn to the left, and then back to the right. It's a good plan, but I can't visualize Margy making the turn without having to back up a few times. And backing up with the quad trailer isn't her specialty. ·

"Why don't you park it for us?" I suggest to John. Margy is stopped now, hesitating before continuing. John and I stand in the place where John wants her to park, ready to guide her into position.

John seems relieved by my suggestion. It will certainly speed up the process. I give Margy the "halt" sign with my raised hand. John walks quickly to her truck. As soon as Margy is out of the driver's door, John bolts into the cab. He swings the truck's trailer in a perfect arc, ending in a straight and level position, facing back down the road.

As John goes back to his own truck and prepares to off-load his quad, I spring into action. We're ahead of the game now, but we could fall behind fast. So I begin unfastening our quad cargo straps, lower the loading ramps, turn on the fuel valves, and begin strapping snow-shoes and poles onto the front of our bikes. John walks over from his truck with his snowshoes in-hand.

"Can you carry my shoes?" he asks. "I need the space for the chainsaw. Could be a lot of downed trees after that storm."

"Sure," I reply. "Put them over there, and I'll strap them onto my bike." My quad can easily carry John's wooden snowshoes and our poles, with Margy's bike carrying our metal snowshoes. So I readjust our loads and hop on my quad to start my engine.

"Get your bike started, so it can warm up," I suggest to Margy, before hitting my own starter switch. She nods "Yes," an indication she understands my haste to keep up with John. But before she is aboard her quad, and before I have backed off the trailer, John is sitting on his quad next to us. His engine is running, helmet on, with Bro already loaded into his riding box. John looks up at me as he adjusts his gloves.

"Almost ready?" he asks.

Our quads are still on the trailer, the snowshoe equipment is barely strapped on, and my bike is still warming up. Margy is fumbling with her jacket and gloves and hasn't even started her engine for the off-load. Ready? – Not even close.

* * * * *

$\mathbf{A}$fter passing the stop sign on the dirt road at Okeover, my overheat light comes on. It's the second time this has happened. On the last trip, the red light came on near the end of the ride. Finally parked back at the airport, I checked the water reservoir level (seemed a little low), added some water, and thought no more about it. Today we are at the beginning of our ride, about to enter Theodosia, so I am more concerned.

I catch up with John, as he waits impatiently at the trail entrance leading to Theodosia. He's obviously in a rush to move on, so this is not the time to tell him I've been delayed while squandering time writing in my notebook (for this chapter) and taking photos. So I'm glad we have the overheat light to discuss instead. John is concerned. An overheat light is not to be taken lightly.

We check the water reservoir level (seems a bit low again) and add some water. We also check the oil level (looks fine).

"You really shouldn't keep going with that light on," says John. "It might be only a bad sensor, but it could be your thermostat or something even worse."

We discuss our options. John reluctantly allows me to continue. But if there are any signs of a rough running engine, indicating overheat, it will be time to come to a quick halt.

(The engine runs fine all day, with a persistent overheat light. The next day, John finds a hole in the radiator. He also discovers the culprit – a tiny stick lodged in the corner. The engine is spared, partly because of the cold weather and the short nature of the ride. Lots of stops, allowing the engine to cool down, also helped. I pay a lot more attention to warning lights these days.)

While we have the coolant reservoir access panel off, several quads join us at the intersection. All, of course, have overheat light opinions to offer, and they all differ. Julie and her mom arrive at the junction on their Bruins. It's great fun to meet them here unexpectedly. Margy and I want to talk with them further, but John is in his hurry-up mode. So we cut it short and wave goodbye.

The trail into Theodosia is as muddy and rough as ever. We navigate the park-like narrow trail up to the crest that separates Lancelot Inlet from Theodosia. Then we follow the wide logging road to the large boulders that mark the old barricade, now barely evident. Loggers put the barrier here, to keep us out. Today, an alternate path around the boulders is easily navigated.

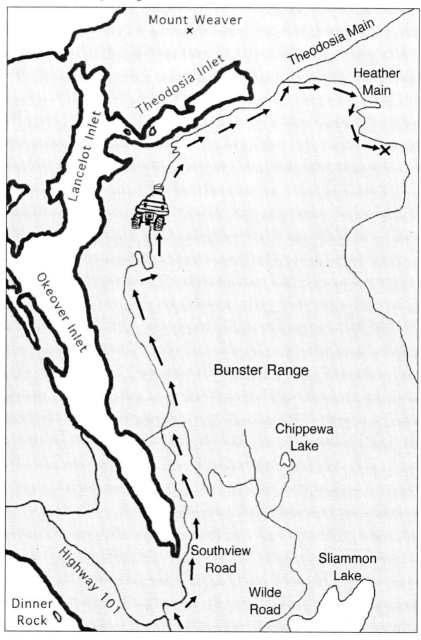

From here, we begin the final descent into the valley. We slip down the last muddy hill and onto the road at the logging camp. The floating barge for the crew's lodging is gone. Logging is in full-swing these days in Theodosia, but the barge-lodge was removed months ago. The loggers are in-and-out each day now. Logging companies don't dismantle logging camps without financial justification, so this must be a sign of increased efficiency.

We travel Theodosia Main to its intersection with Heather Main, where John (always way ahead of us today) waits. He leads us uphill from here. Margy follows on her small Honda, while I ride behind her on my Kodiak. This road extends all the way to Chippewa Bay, but Heather Main can't be driven that far this time of year. The route is notorious for deep snow. So far, for us, the ground is a mix of brown and white.

The tranquil valley below is a nearly continuous stretch of logging cuts. We stop to gaze out over the slashes to the inlet below. John shakes his head. I know what he is thinking. The trees are disappearing everywhere, and no place is it more evident than Theodosia.

John stops at a wide curve in the road where snow completely covers the ground. Margy pulls up behind him and stops. John stands on his quad's running boards and twists to yell something back at her. Still a ways behind, I can't hear anything over the sound of my engine. Margy turns to me, and raises her left gloved-hand high, with four fingers extended. "Four!" – Margy mouths the word, and I understand. John wants me in four-wheel drive from here on. Margy merely relays the message, since her bike has only two-wheel drive. That means she will be the limiting factor in the snow today. Usually, John and I can proceed only a short distance farther than Margy. My driving skills are limited, and John has the burden of blazing the trail on his old, nearly-treadless tires. It seems to even out.

As we climb on Heather Main, the snow gets deeper. We leave the slash and enter the trees. Within less than a kilometer, Margy's rear tires are spinning wildly, but she creeps forward in John's tracks. If she slows down or the road steepens, it is all over. Meanwhile, I watch John in front of her. His tires too are starting to spin, even in four-wheel drive. He is about 100 feet in front of us on the straight-away when he pulls over to the side. Almost simultaneously, Margy grinds to a stop, and I am the only one still going. My newer tires and four-wheel drive provide better traction than John's Grizzly, but by a bare margin. So we are all done riding, nearly simultaneously.

I help Margy rock her light bike to the side of the road, close to the ditch so others can pass. Then I maneuver my bike into position near hers. John has already walked back to retrieve his snowshoes from my rack.

The upward climb from here looks fairly steep. I can imagine what it will feel like on snowshoes. As I don my snowshoes and tighten the straps, the sound of quad engines approaches from below. Two blue Grizzlies driven by a young couple appear around the corner. They're still making good speed up the hill. They slow as they come closer, and then stop momentarily to say "Hi!" Of course, John knows them. As we talk, I notice their extra-large tires. The two Grizzlies then continue up the road with seemingly good traction. In snow like this, tread is everything. The blue quads disappear around the corner, and I listen until their engines finally stop about a half-kilometer farther up the road.

Finally, Margy and I are ready to go, but John is already gone, out of sight around the corner. When we finally catch up with him, he is talking with the young couple near their quads at the side of the road. Margy and I are nearly out of energy after this short climb, but John is well rested and ready to go. He proceeds ahead of us, striding along beside the couple, while we rest.

Margy and I are underway again in a few minutes, but the three figures on snowshoes (plus Bro in his blue jacket) are getting farther ahead. We watch Bro scamper in front of everyone, sometimes leaping nearly vertically out of the snow. His energy is boundless, as he runs ahead, then darts off to the side of the road. He investigates something there, and then prances back to join John.

We're not going to catch up with John today on our snowshoes or our quads, so there's no use trying. Our climb upward is through sparkling snow-crusted trees lining a road that has not been traveled since the last snowfall. The surface is ideal for snowshoes. Too bad for us, it's uphill. Even on level ground, snowshoes demand effort.

While climbing, you really feel it. My T-shirt, under two long-sleeve shirts and my jacket, is now soaked. The atmosphere of the pristine, sparkling snow-scape is cold, but we are plenty warm beneath our winter clothing.

Snowshoes are so different from other modes of travel. They provide entry into a winter wonderland, fresh and glistening, far removed from civilization. The snow is new and natural, such a beautiful sight. We puff and pant without complaint, forcing our bodies to persist in the ascent, as we absorb and cherish the snowy climb.

◊ ◊ ◊ ◊ ◊ ◊ ◊

Chapter 18

False Spring

I t's the first day of spring, and the weather is playing a deceptive trick. It's easy to applaud the sunny skies. But to believe the change is permanent is to accept the short-term as reality. Spring doesn't break here – it eases in over a two-month period.

Two days ago it was rainy and cold. It has been that way for four months, with few respites. Days like today have been infrequent, but not unexpected. It can't rain forever.

What's different about today is the temperature. Yesterday the sun swept the thermometer up to 11 degrees C. Today's prediction calls for a balmy 13 degrees, under clear skies. The long-range forecast is for one more sunny day, and then a return to the rain. Spring will come, but it doesn't necessarily begin with the printed calendar. The process is gradual. Today is a hint of the warm and sunny months to come, eventually.

Even with a daytime temperature that reminds me of spring, the nights are long enough to drop to freezing. Last night, under clear skies, it hit minus 1. By sunrise, frost covered the Campion's canvas cover and the deck of Cabin Number 3.

The first day of spring – the magic date when daytime exactly equals night. From here, daylight gradually overtakes darkness. It marks a significant shift of the seasons, even if the rains move back in tomorrow.

It has been nearly impossible to leave the float cabin the last few days. It is never easy to leave this place I love so much. But sunny days are even more difficult. Yesterday was clear, warm, and tranquil. I launched the tin boat and whipped around the Hole. Then I darted across to Goat Island, and down First Narrows to Sandy Beach. It was still plenty cold at full throttle, but I didn't need a ski mask.

While I played, Margy worked in her floating garden, tilling soil she has rejuvenated with peat moss and manure. Winter rains leach out the nutrients. Water continuously drains through the soil bed and its floating foundation.

On the deck of the cabin, dozens of yogurt containers containing freshly-planted seeds sit in the sun, preparing themselves for transplant into the garden. Margy rotates these containers around the float every few hours, following the low-riding path of the sun. Next week, if weather permits, the floating garden will be planted. Last year, we planted in the rain because we had to leave for the States before the sunshine cooperated. This year, we'd like to plant in the sun, but it's far from guaranteed.

* * * * *

We motor down the lake, basking in the morning light. Spring has sprung (for now), although the Campion's full-canvas cover is still snapped in place over the boat's interior. In another month, it will be removed. Then, while Margy drives, I'll kick back in the front of the bowrider. Stretched out in the bow on a warm, sunny day is one of my favorite indulgences. I can't wait.

At the condo in town, we dress for a day on the chuck. We exchange Margy's truck for my rusty 1987 Ford Tempo with the yellow banana (two-person sea kayak) on top. I've driven around town throughout the winter, in rain and snow, with the banana on top. It draws a few stares, particularly in the winter.

Today, pulling out of the condo's dark, covered parking garage, I give the big banana some encouragement:

"Here it comes, Mr. Kayak! Right around this corner – it's finally here. Warm sunshine! Do you feel that, Mr. Kayak? Spring is finally here."

Mr. Kayak doesn't reply, but I know he is smiling, as he basks in the spring sun. After a cold and rainy winter, he's obviously ready for some action.

It's still March, but the weather seems perfect for kayaking. The air is warm, and I look forward to getting back into the kayak again. But kayaking means being in the water as well as on it. It's a day to dress warm and hope to maintain reasonably dry feet.

We launch at Gibson's Beach, next to Sliammon. The tide is ebbing, so it's a long haul to the bottom of the launch ramp. Still, it's a shorter distance to lug a kayak than in the summer, since we easily find parking near the ramp entrance. Today, there are only two other vehicles in the small parking area, which is normally jammed full in summer.

Getting into Mr. Kayak without getting our feet wet is impossible. Margy and I get the kayak floating by wading in a few inches of water. Then I pull the front cockpit close enough to shore so Margy can get in without wading into the deeper water. Then she paddles to the end of the rock jetty, where I enter from the rocks. The water that slips into my neoprene boots is warmer than I expect. In a few minutes, it is forgotten.

Paddling out from shore, the early afternoon sun beams down on us. It feels much warmer than the forecast 13 degrees. I wear a sweatshirt over a T-shirt, with my nylon jacket packed away inside a waterproof bag. Nearly my whole body is covered. Gloves, nylon pants (with long johns), and a hat protect me from the March air. But the big surprise is that I am actually warm as I paddle. It is the perfect temperature for a kayak trip. Occasional drops of water from Margy's paddle splash against my bare wrists. It feels more refreshing than cold.

Another bonus for this off-season jaunt – no recreational boats passing through Malaspina Strait. Today's trip will take us to Harwood Island, a crossing that would be nerve wracking in summer. Today we will be able to cross without worrying that seasonal cruisers (many of them from the States) will consider us to be nothing more than "speed bumps." Being visible in a kayak, in the midst of heavy boat traffic, is a constant concern. But today there is only the occasional fishing boat. Our Canadian flag flies high on its aft-mounted · pole, as a warning sign to remind others we are here. Today, it is not even needed. On the down side, I miss the fun of yelling "Damn Americans!" as the big cruisers go by, smacking at Mr. Kayak with waves from their large wakes.

The sea is nearly calm, with light northwesterly swells that steal a bit of our energy. We paddle towards the sandspit on Harwood's north end, resting often, enjoying the quiet bobbing of the kayak in the nearly-still water. The snow-capped mountains of Vancouver Island hover off the bow. The peaks glitter in the sun, standing proudly above the island's lowlands, and partly covered by puffy cumulus clouds. Texada Island stretches off to our left. The north end of Texada looks like an elephant, with its trunk extended in front of itself, all the way to Blubber Bay.

This voyage to Harwood is a good choice for the first paddle of the year. It's about 4 kilometers to the sandspit. My paddling muscles are in fair shape from cutting and splitting wood this winter, but I still feel the strain in my forearms.

We pause at mid-channel for a rest. The kayak drifts at will, not moving very far. I pull my camera from its waterproof plastic box and take a few pictures. I stretch my legs as best I can in the cramped hull. My feet are confined within the rudder pedal nooks, but I can wiggle my toes.

Now I ponder our potential landing spot on the island. I want to pull out of the water at the sandspit, but there are interesting shoreline formations straight ahead that beg to be explored. From this distance, it looks like a mix of stumps poking out of the water and big logs that are marooned on the beach.

After the mid-channel rest, I use the rudder to aim the kayak towards our revised destination on the island near the log-strewn beach. A small runabout trolls along Harwood's shoreline, left-to-right, paralleling the beach. When we stop paddling for another brief rest, the voices of the boat's fishermen drift across the half-kilometer of water that separates us. Slowly, they pass in front of us, and are soon out of sight around the point.

As we close in on the island, I can now identify the details of the spot we have been aiming for. It's a wide bay, not unlike the shoreline of the rest of Harwood. The dark spots I saw from a distance are rocks, partially exposed at low tide. Logs are strewn about on the gravel beach.

Within 100 feet of the beach, the sea bottom becomes visible, a blend of seaweed and sand. The water is still quite deep, at least 30 feet. But the clarity is superb, so it looks a lot shallower than it really is.

Continuing towards the shore, I push the rudder to the right, in order to parallel the beach. We angle northward toward the sandspit, gliding along the shoreline, while looking down at the seafloor only a few feet below. A large orange sun star passes beneath the kayak. Simultaneously, a heron on a rock at water's edge flaps his wings. He swoops away, only to land on another rock about 100 feet ahead. When we catch up with him, he flies off again, and lands again a little ways in front of us. He does this repeatedly, as if he is the officially-designated Harwood Island welcoming committee. He takes his job seriously.

Margy and I paddle slowly, inspecting the beach. We stop paddling every few minutes, gazing down to examine the ocean floor. Paddle and drift, paddle and drift.

The sandspit angles out in front of us, and now the sea bottom takes on a more-rocky appearance. We creep in closer to shore, looking for a good spot to pull the kayak out of the water. It is not possible to bring the kayak to shore without getting wet. I roll up my pant legs and long johns before I step out into the water. As we drag Mr. Kayak to shore, I notice that the water is not a numbing cold. My feet are happy.

We lift the kayak and carry it up to dry ground so the waves on the beach won't crunch the hull against the rocks. After setting Mr. Kayak down, I pull my camera from its watertight box and take some pictures, looking across at Sliammon and the paper mill. It's a beautiful day in spring, even if it is a false arrival of the new season.

We walk across the spit to the opposite shore. The beach has a sharper slope on this side, and waves are breaking here with teasing force.

During our stay on the spit, I spend most of my time relaxing on a log stranded midway between the two high-tide marks. It's a narrow corridor, less than 10 feet wide.

The view looking towards the mainland is glorious. The Bunster Range, Goat Island, and Mount Mahony merge into the line of coastal mountains. Behind this frontal line, mountains near the head of Powell Lake poke upward, dominated by Beartooth's sharp triangular summit. To the east, glaciated peaks strike skyward. One of these summits is particularly rugged and massively white. I check the landmarks and realize I'm looking at Mount Alfred, 50 kilometers away.

While I relax on my log, Margy walks inland to explore the edge of the forest. She returns to report finding a huge logging winch, partly overgrown with brush. She is surprised when I don't desire to hike to see the winch myself. It's too lazy a day for me – I'll wait to see her photos instead.

On the paddle back to Gibson's Beach, we pause to view the coastline as we drift silently in nearly flat ocean. The gentle northwesterly wind is barely noticeable, but it pushes our kayak slowly towards land. After we stop paddling, our bow wave is still visible for several minutes, angling off from the front of Mr. Kayak.

We spend considerable time just bobbing on the ocean, gazing at Sliammon. This is a First Nations village, set in a grand location. As I stare at Sliammon, I wonder if the children of this village appreciate their unique and precious location. They look out across the ocean, with breath-taking views of Harwood, Savary, and Vancouver Island. On this warm, spring day, scenery in every direction is a treasure.

* * * * *

Overnight, clouds roll in, and the air is significantly colder the next day. As I leave the grocery store in the late morning, it starts to rain and the wind begins to blow. A few minutes after 2 PM, the Pacific Weather Center of Environment Canada issues a gale warning for the Strait of Georgia. Grief Point's 4:37 PM automated weather report announces 25-knot winds from the east, gusting to 35. The taste of spring is gone, and it is temporarily winter once again.

Epilogue

Out Like a Lamb

It is the end of March, only a week after the first day of spring, and the sky is sunny – again. This could be another bout with false spring, although this time it feels different. The birds are back. Today I watch Stellar's Jays flit from cliff to cliff, stopping briefly to display their striking blue plumage.

This morning, the woodpecker on the fir tree above the cabin was on the job at 6 AM. His territorial singing-cry precedes his rat-tat-tat, as a warning that he is about to hammer. He's been working on this tree for several days. This coincides with the return of a variety of other birds, including swallows, now singing and flying about within the Hole.

After his earlier wakeup call, the woodpecker stops his work. He seems content to rest until his next barrage during the afternoon. That's when his disciplined heavy-work shift begins, with prolonged bouts of rat-tat-tat, rat-tat-tat.

The resident raven is more active too. During the winter I sighted him occasionally, most often identified by the flapping of his large wings. It's a sound I sometimes mistake for the robust strum of the wind generator's hefty blades – whoosh, whoosh. But now Mr. Raven is more aggressive, landing on the deck to investigate the shiny plastic wrap that covers the seedling containers that bask in the sun.

The garden is almost fully planted now. Today it exhibits a dry, tan appearance. Warm rays of the sun penetrate the soil. "Warm," by definition this time of year, means temperatures in the low teens. It feels like the mid-20s, until the sun goes behind the clouds. The garden's yellow daffodils are in full bloom, and a variety of wildflowers are beginning to poke out on some of the cliff ledges. Star-shaped yellow Stonecrop, my personal favorite, can't be far behind.

The air is different. Spring feels more permanent now. A few patches of snow remain on the top of Goat. In the Notch, late afternoon sunlight reaches the ravine's depths. It penetrates the narrow canyon for only a few minutes before the setting sun drapes the Notch in darkness again.

A new waterfall on one of Goat's lower cliffs emerged a few days ago. But it has already dried. It is now only visible as a dark brown 50-foot rut that was momentarily filled by water, as a mountain creek found a more direct route down the cliff. I wonder if this new trench is established well enough to become a recurring waterfall during the next rain. For now, it leaves a natural scar on the landscape.

The weather has changed in the past week. It's not easily measured, but it is obvious to anyone who has spent the winter on the lake. After four months of rain and wind, the past few days have a different flavor: showers, followed by a mix of sun and clouds. It's a welcome change.

I've moved the firewood float from its winter position between the cabin and the cliff. The firewood has been convenient there, floating within quick reach of the patio door during the cold winter months.

And it was a good spot to capture and cut logs that drifted into the Hole. But now, the lake level is dropping fast. Soon the firewood float could jam against the shore. So I have moved it to the end of the long dock, where it will be gradually refilled during the warmer months, ready again for next winter.

The higher mountains are still snow-covered, but melting is accelerating. A truck or quad could now climb above the gravel pit on A-Branch. Soon we will be able to drive all the way to the ski cabin. The winter trails are transitioning into spring paths, many of them now muddy and temporarily impassible. But they will dry into trails that lead into completely different adventures in a new season.

Spring follows winter in a way that is difficult to capture with human logic. When it is cold and rainy, it seems the sun will never shine again. But it does. Then it is all too easy to forget both the challenges and beauties of the cold and wet.

◊ ◊ ◊ ◊ ◊ ◊

About the Author

Author (right) with Powell River Mayor Stewart Alsgard at dedication of Coast Guard's 47-foot *Cape Caution* in Westview Marina, September 2005

From 1980 to 2005, Wayne Lutz held the position of Chairman of the Aeronautics Department at Mount San Antonio College in Los Angeles. He led the college's Flying Team to championships as Top Community College in the United States seven times. He has also served 20 years as a U.S. Air Force C-130 aircraft maintenance office.

The author is a flight instructor with 7000 hours of flying experience. In the past three decades, he has spent summers in Canada, exploring remote regions in his Piper Arrow and camping next to his airplane.

Wayne resides in a floating cabin on Canada's Powell Lake and in a city-folk condo in Los Angeles. His writing genres include regional Canadian publications and science fiction. The author's next book, *Up the Strait,* is scheduled for release in June 2007.

Up the Lake
Up the Main
Up the Winter Trail
Up the Strait

Order books and Photo CDs at:
www.PowellRiverBooks.com

Free Audio Chapters for the first 4 books
in this series are now available at the
Powell River Books web site

Reader's can email the author at:
wlutz@mtsac.edu

Up the Winter Trail is the third is a series
of volumes focusing on the unique geography
and people of coastal British Columbia

Order at: *www.PowellRiverBooks.com*

$5 Instant Rebate

◇ This offer pertains to all books in the UP THE LAKE series
◇ Rebate applies to books purchased at the Powell River
  Books web site – not applicable to in-store retail sales

Rebate details available at:
   http://www.PowellRiverBooks.com/rebate.html

ISBN 141208874-7

140-3